Circular Economy and the Law

This book explores the role of law and policy in circular economy transitions and their impacts on justice, including on distributional equity and recognition and procedural rights, especially for people already marginalised under the current dominant economic system.

Amid increasing demand for virgin raw materials, and unsustainable consumption and waste disposal that are driving the global ecological and climate crisis, there are growing calls to urgently transition to circular economies. Despite an increasing number of circular approaches being adopted, implemented, and integrated in national and local laws and policies, the number of commercially successful business stories remains isolated. Moreover, questions about whether circular economy laws and policies are delivering fair and just global outcomes need to be addressed. This book examines this significant knowledge gap to understand legal experiences, including justice and equity issues in the global context, so that these can inform wider design and implementation. The book begins by explaining the concept of a circular economy and its context within wider issues of sustainable development and justice. The first part of the book then examines the legal context of the circular economy by analysing legal forms in practice and those recommended in wider scholarship before considering how these could impact on existing inequity and injustices globally. The second part delivers an empirical understanding of the implications of the law on circular economy approaches and the global equity and justice dimensions through two case studies on solid waste management and forestry. The final part addresses legal opportunities and challenges for wider implementation of circular economy approaches that incorporate justice into its framing.

This book will be of great interest to students, scholars, and practitioners of environmental and natural resource law and policy, circular economy, industrial ecology, natural resource management, and sustainable development more broadly.

Feja Lesniewska is a Lecturer and Research Fellow in the Institute for Sustainable Resources and UCL Laws at University College London, UK. She holds a PhD in Sustainable Development and International Law from SOAS University of London, UK.

Katrien Steenmans is a Postdoctoral Researcher at the Centre for Private Governance (CEPRI) in the Faculty of Law at Copenhagen University, Denmark. She holds a PhD in Environmental Law from the University of Surrey, UK.

Routledge Focus on Environment and Sustainability

For more information about this series, please visit: www.routledge.com/Routledge-Focus-on-Environment-and-Sustainability/book-series/RFES

Circular Economy and the Law

Bringing Justice into the Frame

Feja Lesniewska and Katrien Steenmans

 Routledge
Taylor & Francis Group

LONDON AND NEW YORK

 from Routledge

First published 2023
by Routledge
4 Park Square, Milton Park, Abingdon, Oxon OX14 4RN

and by Routledge
605 Third Avenue, New York, NY 10158

Routledge is an imprint of the Taylor & Francis Group, an informa business

British Library Cataloguing-in-Publication Data
A catalogue record for this book is available from the British Library

Library of Congress Cataloging-in-Publication Data
Names: Lesniewska, Feja, author. | Steenmans, Katrien, author.
Title: Circular economy and the law : bringing justice into the frame /
Feja Lesniewska and Katrien Steenmans.
Description: New York, NY : Routledge, 2023. | Includes
bibliographical references and index.
Identifiers: LCCN 2022041096 (print) | LCCN 2022041097 (ebook) |
ISBN 9780367375331 (hardback) | ISBN 9781032436586 (paperback) |
ISBN 9780429355141 (ebook)
Subjects: LCSH: Circular economy. | Environmental policy. |
Environmental justice. | Sustainability.
Classification: LCC GE170 .L476 2023 (print) | LCC GE170 (ebook) |
DDC 363.7/0561—dc23/eng20221209
LC record available at https://lccn.loc.gov/2022041096
LC ebook record available at https://lccn.loc.gov/2022041097

ISBN: 978-0-367-37533-1 (hbk)
ISBN: 978-1-032-43658-6 (pbk)
ISBN: 978-0-429-35514-1 (ebk)

DOI: 10.4324/9780429355141

Typeset in Times New Roman
by codeMantra

Contents

Figure

Tables

Preface

Research interest in the circular economy is growing exponentially as people are drawn to what is perceived to be a viable alternative to the dominant linear unsustainable economic model driving the triple planetary ecological crises of climate change, mass biodiversity extinction, and ecosystem degradation. Identifying pathways to circular economy transitions that reduce pressure on the planet's resources, contribute to climate change mitigation, and support resilient ecosystem recovery are priorities in research across multiple disciplines from engineering to law and policy. Missing from the research agenda on circular economy transitions is social justice and the effects any changes to existing economic legal systems could have. With this in mind, we chose to write this book to bring justice into the frame of research on law and the circular economy.

The initial idea behind this book was to collate and analyse circular economy laws from around the world as such research was yet to be published. However, we were conscious that legal research on the circular economy had yet to consider the social aspects of a transition away from a linear economy. Although there were signs that the situation was beginning to change the quality and rate at which research on justice, law, and the circular economy transition was taking place, we found this inadequate compared with other areas that focus on regulatory mechanisms such as extended producer responsibility, circular design labelling, and rent-for-service contracts.

Inevitably in a book of this length we have had to be selective in our coverage and focus. The book is intended to initiate a shift towards an increased focus on equity and justice issues within circular economy legal research. A great deal more research will be needed to truly situate justice at the centre of law and circular economy research, and feed into law and policy-making in practice.

We also have several people that we wish to thank. Our families – Feja (Lisa and Benji) and Katrien (Phil, Ada, Daphne, Ollie, Chris, Gerd, Ine, Lore, Christian, and Sheila) – all contributed in their own way. They helped with proofreading and feedback, but most valued was their support in providing us time and space to finish this book. We also express our thanks to our editors and Routledge for their patience and ongoing support throughout this project. Finally, we thank each other. Our collaboration has spanned changing professional and personal circumstances during which we have forged a friendship.

Feja Lesniewska and Katrien Steenmans

Abbreviations

BE	Bioeconomy
BECCS	Bioenergy carbon capture and storage
CBD	Convention on Biological Diversity
CE	Circular economy
CFBE	Circular forest bioeconomy
COP	Conference of the parties
EMF	Ellen MacArthur Foundation
EPR	Extended producer responsibility
EU	European Union
FSC	Forest Stewardship Council
GDP	Gross domestic product
IPCC	Intergovernmental Panel on Climate Change
IRP	International Resource Panel
LULUCF	Land use, land use change and forestry
NET	Negative emissions technologies
PET	Polyethylene terephthalate
RED	Renewable Energy Directive
REDD+	Reduced emissions from deforestation and degradation
SDGs	Sustainable Development Goals
UN	United Nations
UNCLOS	United Nations Convention on the Law of the Sea
UNEA	United Nations Environmental Assembly
UNEP	United Nations Environment Programme
UNFCCC	United Nations Framework Convention on Climate Change

1 Introduction

1.1 Introduction

Current global resource consumption and waste production levels are unsustainable and contribute to increasing ecosystem degradation. Annual global primary resource use is outpacing population growth and has exceeded 100 billion tonnes per year as of 2019 (OECD 2018; Circle Economy 2022). The International Resource Panel (IRP) estimates that by 2050 this annual global material use figure could reach 184 billion tonnes (IRP 2017). Such increasing material use will take the world beyond identified planetary boundaries, potentially making the Earth's environment unfit for humans and many millions of other species (Steffen et al. 2015). Simultaneously, production and consumption processes result in more than two billion tonnes of municipal solid waste annually, which could almost double to 3.4 billion tonnes by 2050 (Kaza et al. 2018). The levels of waste globally pose significant threats to human health and ecosystem resilience, although the burdens are not distributed equitably (UNEP and ISWA 2015).

Many concepts have been developed or adopted to address the resource and waste crises, including sustainable development, green economy, resource efficiency, and resource nexus. This book is devoted to the concept of the circular economy (CE), which has recently gained prominence in academia, the private sector, and amongst government policy-makers (Gregson et al. 2015). In essence, the CE aims to move away from a linear take-make-dispose model of resource use towards the prevention of waste and looping any wastes produced and other resources through reuse, recycling, and other recovery (see Section 1.2).

The CE concept has been lauded for its anticipated economic, environmental, and social benefits, though its possible contributions for low- and middle-income countries of the Global South (except for

DOI: 10.4324/9780429355141-1

China) have so far received relatively little attention (Schroeder et al. 2019). For example, Accenture has estimated that the financial rewards of CE business models could reach USD 4.5 trillion by 2030 (Lacy and Rutqvist 2015). Expected economic gains in Europe and China from transitioning towards CEs are claimed to be in the region of EUR 1.8 trillion by 2030 and more than USD 10 trillion by 2040, respectively (Ellen MacArthur Foundation and McKinsey Centre for Business and Environment 2015; Arup and Ellen MacArthur Foundation 2018). A global CE is also predicted to have the potential to be instrumental in the drive to mitigate certain resource-related climate impacts, given that the majority (67 percent) of global greenhouse gas emissions are related to material management (Circle Economy 2020). Identified social benefits from CEs are largely focused on job creation (see Section 1.3.1). For instance, Cambridge Econometrics et al. (2018) predict that CE activities could create around 700,000 net additional jobs within Europe. Such predicted employment gains from transitioning to a CE are, however, uncertain and contested. If CEs are to support Sustainable Development Goal (SDG) targets, the evidence base of CEs and their expected value gains need to be extended.

Despite the multiple proclaimed benefits, the world's CEs are yet to develop and mature. Indeed, the 'circularity gap', i.e., the amount of resources extracted compared to the amount of material loss due to waste generation and stock depletion, is actually increasing (Circle Economy 2022; Kunzig 2020). Currently, only 8.6 percent of resources and materials in the global economy are reused and recycled (Circle Economy 2020). Meanwhile, there are only a few isolated successful CE business cases (Mathews and Tan 2016), many of which are described as 'limited and fragile' (Gregson et al. 2015).

To enable a more rapid transition to a CE, it is widely recognised that government support and legislation are necessary (Agamuthu et al. 2009; Moktadir et al. 2018). Even though lawyers, policy-makers, and academics are engaged with questions about the role law and policy needs to play to enable a CE, the approach adopted lacks a critical dimension (Genovese and Pansera 2019). Questions about the impact laws will have on distributional equity and justice, and how a CE will avoid repeating injustices the linear economic legal infrastructure created and has sustained, are largely missing from the research agenda. This book is the first to explore the range of CE-related laws being adopted globally as well as critically consider the implications those laws will have on the world's justice terrain, historic, current, and future. The book demonstrates that if a just, inclusive CE is to be created, existing inequities and injustices need not only to be understood, especially the role that laws have played in embedding them within the linear economic system, but also acted upon.

The remainder of this chapter sets out the book's conceptual framework and key arguments beginning in Section 1.2 with the origins of the CE as a concept. Following on in Section 1.3, CE definitions are discussed and a number of conceptual challenges outlined including waste, waste management operations, sustainable development, scale, and social justice for current and future generations. The chapter concludes in Section 1.4 with a summary and chapter overviews.

1.2 Origins of the Circular Economy

Even though the explicit labelling of the CE concept has been developed recently, its fundamental essence of preventing waste being 'wasted' and reusing, recycling, and recovery of wastes and resources is not new. There is no wasted waste in ecosystems. In certain regions, for example, the dropping of leaves by deciduous trees in autumn may be viewed as the disposal of leaves (Davis 2020). The leaves are, however, not wasted as they decompose and become nutrients for the soil. It is thus not that waste does not exist or is not produced in nature, but instead that nothing is wasted and everything is a resource. Anthropologists have also documented numerous examples of similar approaches to waste as a resource since time immemorial. For example, an Indonesian folktale, where a farmer heard sobbing coming from her field and finds that it belongs to a handful of rice plants that were left behind during the harvest in the rice paddy, is recounted to children to teach them about not wasting food (Soma 2016); in Aotearoa New Zealand, Te Ao Māori has for centuries provided a roadmap for a system of production and trade of goods and services that is centred around long-term community and environmental outcomes (Greenwood et al. 2018); and between the 16th and 20th centuries in Japan, whole whale carcasses were used with any waste being avoided (Institute of Cetacean Research 2007).

Debates over the origin of the CE concept, however, began much more recently. Murray et al. (2017) surveyed various debates (see also Gregson et al. 2015), including some attributing CE to the first President of the Royal Society of Chemistry, RW Hofmann, who in 1848 stated that 'in an ideal chemical factory there is, strictly speaking, no waste but only products'; while Greyson (2007) identifies Kenneth Boulding's (1966) *The Economics of the Coming Spaceship Earth*; whereas Gregson et al. (2015) claim the CE starts with the theories of classical economists Malthus and Ricardo resurfacing in response to

Rachel Carson's (1962) *Silent Spring* and Boulding's work. Many of the CE origin debates are predominantly Western-centric, but Murray et al. (2017) have also identified scholars that claim it is a Chinese concept; Yuan et al. (2006) attribute the first proposal of the CE concept to an article by Zhu in 1998.[1] Similarly, Liu et al. (2009) also attribute it to 1998, but do not credit a particular scholar.

These origin debates are further complicated because many schools of thought are identified as providing the foundation for CE principles (see e.g., Lewandowski 2016; Millar et al. 2019). For example, Stahel and Reday-Mulvey (1976) referred to a closed-loop system; Frosch and Gallopoulos (1989) popularised the field of industrial ecology, which they developed as analogous to biological ecosystems that conserve and reuse resources; and McDonough and Braungart (2002) have advocated cradle-to-cradle design models since the 1990s, which aim to maintain the status of materials as resources by viewing materials as nutrients within biological and technical metabolisms. Other schools of thought that have been identified as CE precursors include environmental economics, industrial ecosystems, cleaner production, product-service systems, biomimicry, the performance economy, regenerative design, and complex utilisation.

The epistemological shift away from inherent indigenous concepts of circularity began with European industrialisation in the 18th century. Up to the 18th century, the problem economies faced was largely how to maximise natural resource use where under-exploitation was prevalent. With industrialisation, which was powered by fossil fuels (that over time has significantly contributed to the contemporary planetary climate change crisis), the problem increasingly became one of managing the unsustainable over-exploitation of natural resource use (Wolloch 2017). Political economists at the time, for example Adam Smith, provided the new economic concepts such as the division of labour, economies of scale, and the limited company, that became the bedrock of global economic, investment, trade, and company law.

1.3 The Circular Economy Concept

The different origins and conceptual roots of the CE explain in part why there are so many definitions, both in academic and practitioner literature. Kovacic et al. (2019) concluded that CE is 'a lot of things at the same time while also being different things in different places' (see also Section 2.2). Kirchherr et al. (2017) reviewed 114 scholarly and practitioner definitions to provide a conceptual foundation for further research on the CE:

an economic system that is based on business models which replace the "end-of-life" concept with reducing, alternatively reusing, recycling and recovering materials in production/distribution and consumption processes, thus operating at the micro level (products, companies, consumers), meso level (eco-industrial parks) and macro level (city, region, nation and beyond), with the aim to accomplish sustainable development, which implies creating environmental quality, economic prosperity and social equity, to the benefit of current and future generations.

(Kirchherr et al. 2017)

In the following subsections, we briefly consider the five key elements in Kirchherr et al.'s framing of the CE: (1) waste, (2) prevention, reuse, recycling, or recovery of resources and wastes, (3) for the purpose of sustainable development, (4) at any scale, and (5) to create social equity for the benefit of current and future generations. Kirchherr et al.'s framing is returned to in the analysis of the two case studies in Chapter 6.

1.3.1 Waste

Central to the CE concept is waste. Much literature already exists on defining waste (e.g., Cheyne and Purdue 1995; Scotford 2007). For our purposes, the understanding of waste as comprising materials, which one disposes of, intends to dispose of, or is required to be disposed of, is sufficient. This reflects the waste definition within the Basel Convention on the Control of Transboundary Movements of Hazardous Wastes and Their Disposal (Basel Convention)[2] and the EU's Waste Framework Directive (2008/98/EC).[3] The physical act of disposing may occur through, for instance, placing materials in waste receptacles such as bins. Requirements to dispose are often in law, for example the Basel Convention relies on national provisions (Art. 2(1)), and also frequently straightforward, such as Art. 10 of the Joint Convention on the Safety of Spent Fuel Management and on the Safety of Radioactive Waste Management states that contracting parties may require the disposal of spent fuel (i.e., nuclear fuel that has been irradiated in and permanently removed from a reactor core). Intention is, however, the least clear: What constitutes intent? Who determines whether there is intent? If there is an intention to dispose of an object, but the waste holder and owner changes their mind, does the object briefly become waste and then a reused good? In Germany's Circular Economy Act (see Chapter 2), these components are detailed.

The Act not only adopts the definition of waste set out in the EU Waste Framework Directive (2008/98/EC) but also includes a definition for 'discard', 'a desire to discard', the contribution of the waste producer's or holder's opinion in determining whether an object or substance is waste, and describes when the holder must discard substances or objects (s. 3(1)–(3)).

Arguably, the CE concept means that acts, intentions, and requirements of disposal should occur very little, and that the concept of waste should therefore almost become redundant and meaningless beyond inevitable and unavoidable waste (see Section 1.3.2); in CEs, wastes should not be disposed and there should be no intent to dispose of waste, as the intent would be to reuse, recycle, or recover the material or substance. This is, however, more complex in certain jurisdictions. In the EU, C-418/97-C-419/97 *ARCO Chemie*[4] concluded that a substance undergoing a common method of recovery may indicate that a substance is waste (para 69).[5] The significance of the term 'waste' is also a moot issue as it does not notably impact the production and consumption processes, but only the legal labelling. Instead, the focus should be on a change to physical consumption and production issues, which should be at the heart of the CE concept and is also why the definition of the CE in this book covers both wastes and resources.

1.3.2 Prevention, Reuse, Recycling, and Recovery

Prevention, reuse, recycling, and recovery are central actions of and within CEs. Prevention requires proactive action before resources are consumed or waste is produced, while reuse, recycling, and recovery are all reactive actions once waste has been created. Generally, reuse entails use without processing, but can, for example, include repairing, such as remanufacturing, refurbishment, or cleaning; recycling covers the reprocessing of wastes into other products and materials; and recovery is any other operation that uses waste to replace other materials in a process, including energy recovery. For example, if the intention is to discard a shirt and is therefore considered waste within certain legal regimes, the use of it as a rag for cleaning is an example of reuse, using it as a material to make a tote bag, pillowcase, or belt is considered recycling, and burning it to produce heat falls under recovery.

In ideal CEs, no waste is produced and resource use is minimised because waste prevention is prioritised. However, in all CEs, some resource inputs remain necessary, as a result of quality losses and energy requirements (Velenturf et al. 2020). Only where prevention and minimisation cannot be achieved should wastes and resources be reused, recycled, or recovered. Many argue that in practice prevention is not prioritised, as the focus in regulation and policy is predominantly on recycling (Ghisellini et al. 2016; Kirchherr et al. 2017).

Numerous CE business models of multinational companies remain growth orientated. The Coca-Cola Company and Amazon, for example, have both promoted their commitments to a CE, but the Coca-Cola Company focuses on designing packaging from recycled materials and recycling bottles and cans, and Amazon is focused on increasing recycling and providing reuse and repair initiatives (Coca-Cola Company 2021; Amazon 2021). This raises the question of to what extent such multinational companies can be truly 'circular', as current business models and the economic system incentivises continued consumption and therefore essentially 'same-but-circular-business' models. Furthermore, in promoting the closing of loops in which waste is perpetually returned to business (e.g., in industrial symbiosis – see Section 4.3.2), waste is often commodified, as a result of being sold in secondary markets, and becomes embedded in the economic system (Ferguson and Souza 2010; Steenmans and Malcolm 2020). The consequence of commodification is that the incentive to change the system to reduce and prevent waste is lost.

1.3.3 Sustainable Development

Sustainable development is frequently included as an objective for CE in both academic and practitioner literature (e.g., Ghisellini et al. 2016; Kirchherr et al. 2017). The sustainable dimension of the CE concept, however, is problematic for several reasons.

First, the relationship between CE and sustainable development in academic and wider literature has not yet been thoroughly explored or defined. It seems to be commonly accepted that a linear take-make-dispose economy cannot lead to sustainable development (e.g., Frosch and Gallopoulos 1989; Costanza et al. 2014). As such it is assumed that CEs will by default result in sustainable development. Scholars caution that despite the patent similarities, the concepts should not be conflated as CE is a subset of sustainability with actions central to CE deemed necessary for sustainable development (Ghisellini et al. 2016; Geissdoerfer et al. 2017; Kirchherr et al. 2017). Beyond this link being superficially recognised, there are no reviews on how CE can be a tool for sustainable development (Millar et al. 2019), except for Korhonen et al. (2018) who limited their discussion to CE and environmental sustainability. Also, Schroeder et al. (2019) and Rodriguez-Anton et al. (2019) have both concluded that CE practices can potentially contribute to achieving some of the SDG (see below) targets. Yet more evidence is still needed as current research on the ability of CEs to benefit SDGs relies on multiple contested assumptions (Millar et al. 2019).

Second, there are challenges in relation to the concept of sustainable development itself (Kotzé and Adelman 2022). Sustainable development as an aim of CE is usually understood by adopting the three-pillared approach of economic, environmental, and social dimensions (Kirchherr et al. 2017). The three-pillared approach has resulted in questions (Ross 2009; Kallis 2011; Jackson 2016), including: Is it possible to achieve economic growth, social justice, and environmental benefits concurrently? If a balanced approach is not possible between the three strands, which one takes priority? Is continued economic growth desirable? Some of the criticisms of the sustainable development concept were intended to be addressed by the UN SDGs set in 2015. The 17 SDGs cover, for example, climate action, affordable and clean energy, and gender equality, and aim to achieve a better and more sustainable future for all (United Nations 2015). Target 12.5 of SDG 12 on ensuring sustainable consumption and production states that waste generation should be substantially reduced by 2030 through prevention, reduction, recycling, and reuse, which are directly supportive of the CE concept. Even though they are described as 'integrated and indivisible and balanc[ing] the three dimensions of sustainable development' (United Nations 2015, preamble), in practice they are criticised for being vague, weak, meaningless, and lacking coherence (ICSU and ISSC 2015; Kim 2016; Holden et al. 2017).

It is increasingly recognised that the current linear economic model is fundamentally unsustainable and there is a need to at the very least decouple economic growth from environmental impacts. However, research shows that there is as yet no empirical evidence to prove that decoupling exists anywhere on the scale required to prevent breaching planetary boundaries (Parrique et al. 2019; Hickel and Kallis 2020). Many consider a paradigm shift is required in economic theory and practice. Various initiatives and scholarly fields exist for this purpose, including green growth (Wiedmann et al. 2020), ecological economics (Daly and Farley 2011), doughnut economics (Raworth 2017), and degrowth (Demaria et al. 2013). For CE to disrupt rather than foster the status quo, it is imperative that it engages with and draws on existing and emerging alternative economic theories.

1.3.4 Scale

There are many different scales within an economic system. CEs are no different; they can occur at micro, meso, and/or macro levels. At micro level, for instance, certain retailers accept used clothing for recycling into new clothes, charity shops practices centre around the reuse and recycling of goods, or some private households reuse waste-paper as draft paper. Meso level examples include industrial symbiosis, in which traditionally separate industries and other organisations exchange waste and by-products with economic, environmental, and social benefits (Chertow 2007; see Section 4.3.2), and eco-industrial parks, which is in essence a narrower form of industrial symbiosis where firms are co-located (Peddle 1990; Côté and Hall 1995). At the other end of the spectrum at the macro level, European waste recovered as energy in Swedish district heating systems (Vattenfall 2022) and exports of recyclable wastes from the Global North to Global South can arguably be part of a global CE (Liu et al. 2018).

The multiscale dimension of CE models raises questions in relation to the required environmental standards, and lower and upper boundaries of CEs needed to constitute a circular system: Can a system be partly circular? Does circularity exist on a spectrum? Chertow (2007) introduced a 3:2 heuristic requiring three different entities, of which none are engaged primarily in a recycling-oriented relationship, exchanging at least two different resources. Such heuristic recognises complex relationships rather than one-way exchanges.[6]

Each level across each sector has different social, environmental, and economic impacts. Preference for one level over another can result in material lock-ins that are detrimental to transitioning to a sustainable and just CE in the long term. Industrial symbiosis, for example, is usually only economically viable at the meso level or as part of a wider macro level CE, where foundation industries like steel, (petro)chemicals, cement, and glass rely on large amounts of waste often from other sectors to sustain operating at scale. Demand within industrial symbiosis systems can perpetuate a failure to move up the waste hierarchy towards prevention because of the commercial market for waste it creates. This undermines realising a CE.

Commodifying waste materials can also stimulate oligopolies to form to capture the commercial opportunities at a mega-regional and/or global (macro) scale. Movements of materials to the highest bidder can crowd out opportunities for localised micro scale businesses, who may have innovative uses for materials more aligned with CE principles, to be actors in the market. This is an all too familiar phenomenon within the current global linear economy which is based on free trade and neo-liberal principles. If CEs are to not replicate the concentration of economic power within the meso and macro levels then justice dimensions need to be taken into account.

1.3.5 Social Equity

A key element to Kirchherr et al.'s (2017) CE conceptual framing is the inclusion of 'social equity for current and future generations' as an objective. The CE will have both temporal and spatial impacts on societies around the world. Although advocates increasingly argue that the CE is a win-win-win due to the multiple benefits, such as less pollution, climate change mitigation, and high skilled employment, it remains to be seen exactly how the impacts will play out.

Social equity and related justice aspects of a CE transition are only beginning to be recognised by advocates and considered within law and policy research (see Chapter 3). Yet, focus on social equity within CEs remains superficial compared to the research being undertaken within other fields of environmental and climate justice. Benefits to future generations from how a CE legal order is constituted, have received even less consideration.

Environmental law was a pioneer in developing principles on equity for current and future generations (Weiss 1990). The principles are included in key multilateral agreements including the 1992 UN Framework Convention on Climate Change (UNFCCC) and the 1992 Convention on Biological Diversity (CBD). Environmental law is also a key domain for focusing on redressing historical inequities through the principle of common but differentiated responsibility, a principle which has fed into justice discourse including advancing concepts such as restorative and regenerative justice such as loss and damage under the 2015 UNFCCC Paris Agreement (Robinson and Carlson 2021).

Another important legal domain to address equity for current generations is that of human and indigenous peoples' rights. Adopting a rights-based approach to transitioning to an inclusive CE would open valuable legal avenues to advance equity and justice concerns in policy, but also in the courts. Recognition rights supporting non-discrimination and participatory rights are already well established in human and indigenous peoples' rights law (see Chapter 3). Also, increasingly legal duties are being placed upon businesses to meet human rights obligations in all their activities across their entire value chain.[7] CE could act as a spur to uphold and advance further rights-based approaches through adopting transparent key performance indicators and reporting mechanisms. There are however critiques of rights-based approaches because of the epistemological origins rooted in the Western Enlightenment, which are discussed in Chapter 3.

Without understanding how to equitably distribute the benefits from a transition to a CE within current and future generations, it is likely that any transition will merely perpetuate the status quo of gross inequity and injustices, many of which are long-standing legacies of colonialism (Friant et al. 2020).

1.4 Structure and Chapter Overviews

Before setting out the structure and chapter overviews, it needs to be noted that throughout this book we purposefully refer to 'CE and the law' rather than 'CE law'. CE is neither a discrete and self-contained regime, nor does it sit within the broader context of one particular area of law – though currently it is largely subsumed within environmental law in practice. Instead, the concept's emerging multilevel, multi-actor, and multi-sector nature means that it would at this stage be unhelpful, undesirable, and even detrimental to its development to refer to this field of study as 'CE law'. A comparable example is evidenced with 'climate law', which also has multi-dimensional characteristics. Climate law was initially dominated by climate mitigation research to the exclusion of adaptation, litigation, and loss and damage. For law and the CE, there are similar risks from limiting and narrowing the research frame. What is alarming is that the few existing explicitly labelled CE laws appear already to have limited themselves to a particular area of environmental law – often waste and resource laws (see Chapter 2). Such an approach has resulted in side-lining fundamental CE principles. To avoid perpetuating this pattern, we purposefully in this book adopt the phrase CE and the law.

Chapter 2 provides a foundation for understanding the sprawling field of CE and the law through reviewing the status quo of legal areas and mechanisms supporting CEs and CE transitions broadly. We distinguish between three approaches in the law: (1) explicitly labelled CE laws, (2) laws underpinning CE principles, and (3) laws impacting CEs. In Section 2.2, we review CE definitions and objectives set out in explicitly labelled CE laws and argue that their current substantive measures fail to adequately cover actions beyond waste recovery. Section 2.3 sets out examples of current ways in which laws can underpin CE principles. Laws can support CEs directly by including the CE concept within their objective or by being mandated by an explicitly labelled CE law, whereas indirect links can exist through aligning either with the CE concept's aims or central actions of prevention, reuse, recycling, and recovery of wastes and resources. In Section 2.4, we cover laws beyond environmental law that can and should be integrated under CE and the law to acknowledge the CE concept's broad-ranging nature.

Chapter 3 explores how worldviews and values embedded within the dominant global legal system have a determining influence on social justice issues, for instance, by excluding certain communities from access to resources. A CE created on the back of the dominant legal system could result in perverse outcomes, exacerbating long-standing distributional, recognition, and procedural injustices. Research on equity and justice by critical legal scholars and political ecologists, especially recent studies on environmental and climate change justice, is a valuable resource to critically evaluate law and policy approaches to establishing a CE. In Section 3.2, we set out current legal research's limitations on CE issues, and why justice issues need to be added to the agenda. The following section then outlines current material distributive inequities, as well as the legal roots of injustices. In the final section, Section 3.4, using justice scholarship, especially environmental and climate change, we take stock of distributive, recognition, and procedural justice issues that need to be brought into the frame if law is to enable a just and inclusive CE.

Chapters 4 and 5 focus on two case studies: circular plastics economy and the circular forest bioeconomy (CFBE), respectively. Each case study provides insights into how the CE is being developed within a specific sector and the associated justice implications.

Chapter 4 examines a particular case study of the traditional solid, non-hazardous waste sector focus of CE approaches: plastics. There are ways in which plastic wastes are currently being used circularly through their prevention, reuse, recycling, and other recovery, but many of these have detrimental environmental and social consequences. In Section 4.2, we review existing tensions between the conceptualisation of plastic wastes as a resource versus pollution that draw out some of these issues. The chapter then considers bottom-up and top-down initiatives to incentivise a circular plastics economy. Bottom-up approaches allow for flexibility and elasticity in circular initiatives, whereas top-down governance can implement regulatory interventions to facilitate CE transitions. Section 4.3 covers the informal recycling sector, which can be a major contributor to CEs, and industrial symbiosis, which usually comprises a network of predominantly private stakeholders. Section 4.4 sets out current developments in international plastic waste management with a particular focus on the proposed global treaty on plastic pollution, as well as national measures (being) adopted and proposed for a circular plastics economy. Justice issues are highlighted throughout these two sections. The underlying argument throughout the chapter is that plastics are still approached in a predominantly linear way with circular plastics promoted through solution-based responses to facilitate 'same-but-circular-business' models.

The second case study in Chapter 5 focuses on the CFBE. Although certain CFBE aspects, such as packaging and paper recycling, biomass from forest residues, and forest carbon markets, already exist, an integrated circular system has yet to be established that cascades materials within a maximum value closed loop in accordance with CE principles. In Section 5.2, we first outline definitional issues with the CFBE. Section 5.3 follows with an overview of forest law's historical roots and discussion of interconnections with contemporary issues such as sustainability, ecosystem science, and traditional indigenous peoples' worldviews. The chapter concludes in Section 5.4 with three case studies from within the forest resource sector that form part of a CFBE. Through the case studies, forest carbon sequestration services, timber construction products, and bioenergy tensions are highlighted between achieving sustainable forest management, mitigating climate change, using property rights fairly, guaranteeing ecological integrity, and recognising indigenous peoples' rights within a CFBE. In conclusion, we argue that the CFBE will not be able to deliver an inclusive sustainable circularity if it continues to pursue current law and policy measures without a change to how forests are valued.

Before the conclusions, Chapter 6 presents analysis of the two case studies covered in the preceding two chapters. In Section 6.2, we use Kirchherr et al.'s (2017) conceptual framing of the CE around five themes – (1) waste, (2) prevention, reuse, recycling, or recovery of resources and wastes, (3) sustainable development, (4) scale, and (5) social equity for the benefit of current and future generations – introduced and reviewed in this chapter to highlight some of the limitations of current laws and policies supporting CE transitions within the two case study sectors. The common thread emerging from the case studies across these five themes is that by bringing justice into the framing of CEs, critical challenges and limitations of the CE will come to the fore. Explicit engagement with these issues will facilitate CE implementations that are truly circular and not just 'same-but-circular-business' models.

In Chapter 7, the concluding remarks are accompanied by several points of context – climate change, global trade, governance, and digital technology – that we argue will play a formative role in shaping future CEs through both barriers and opportunities in the coming decades around the world.

Notes

1 Yuan et al. (2006) references Zhu, D. 1998. The circular economy and Shanghai's countermeasures. *Social Sciences*, 10, pp. 13–17.
2 Wastes are defined as 'substances or objects which are disposed of or are intended to be disposed of or are required to be disposed of by the provisions of national law' (Basel Convention, Art. 2(1)).
3 Waste is defined as 'any substance or object which the holder discards or intends or is required to discard' (EU Waste Framework Directive, Art. 3(1)). Only the English definition was changed in 1991 to use the term 'dispose' instead of 'discard', implying that the change was for linguistic rather than substantive reasons (see Steenmans 2018).
4 *ARCO Chemie Nederland Ltd v Minister van Volkshuisvesting, Ruimtelijke Ordening en Milieubeheer, Vereniging Dorpsbelang Hees and Others v Directeur van de dienst Milieu en Water van de Provincie Gelderland* (C-418/97-C-419/97) [2000] ECR I-4475.
5 See Steenmans (2018) for an overview of characteristics indicating whether a substance is waste within the EU.
6 The 3:2 heuristic was introduced in relation to industrial symbiosis.
7 United Nations Guiding Principles on Business and Human Rights adopted by UN Human Rights Council 16 June 2011. See www.ohchr.org/en/business-and-human-rights.

References

Agamuthu P., Khidzir, K.M. and Hamid, F.S. 2009. Drivers of sustainable waste management in Asia. *Waste Management and Research*, 27(7), pp.625–633. https://doi.org/10.1177/0734242X09103191.

Amazon. 2021. Circular economy. https://sustainability.aboutamazon.co.uk/environment/circular-economy.

Arup and Ellen MacArthur Foundation. 2018. *The Circular Economy Opportunity for Urban and Industrial Innovation in China*. https://ellenmacarthurfoundation.org/urban-and-industrial-innovation-in-china.

Boulding, K. 1966. The economics of the coming spaceship Earth. In: Jarrett, H. (Ed.), *Environmental Quality in a Growing Economy*. Resources for the Future/Johns Hopkins University Press.

Cambridge Econometrics, Trinomics and ICF. 2018. *Impacts of Circular Economy Policies on the Labour Market*. European Commission.

Carson, R. 1962. *Silent Spring*. Houghton Mifflin.

Chertow, M. 2007. "Uncovering" industrial symbiosis. *Journal of Industrial Ecology*, 11(1), pp.11–30. https://doi.org/10.1162/jiec.2007.1110.

Cheyne, I. and Purdue, M. 1995. Fitting definition to purpose: the search for a satisfactory definition of waste. *Journal of Environmental Law*, 7(2), pp.149–168. https://doi.org/10.1093/jel/7.2.149.

Circle Economy. 2020. *Circularity Gap Report 2020.* Platform for Accelerating the Circular Economy. www.circularity-gap.world/.

Circle Economy. 2022. *Circularity Gap Report 2022.* Platform for Accelerating the Circular Economy. www.circularity-gap.world/.

Coca-Cola Company. 2021. *Moving Toward a Circular Economy: Responsibly Managing Plastic Waste.* www.coca-colacompany.com/news/moving-toward-a-circular-economy.

Costanza, R., Kubiszewski, I., Giovannini, E. et al. 2014. Development: time to leave GDP behind. *Nature,* 505, pp.283–285. https://doi.org/10.1038/505283a.

Côté, R. and Hall, J. 1995 Industrial parks as ecosystems. *Journal of Cleaner Production,* 3(1), pp.41–46. https://doi.org/10.1016/0959-6526(95)00041-C.

Daly, H.E. and Farley, J. 2011. *Ecological Economics: Principles and Applications.* Island Press.

Davis, R. 2020. *Trees and the Circular Economy.* www.theleafcharity.com/blog/treesandthecirculareconomy.

Demaria, F., Schneider, F. Sekulova, F. and Martinez-Alier. 2013. What is degrowth? From an activist slogan to a social movement. *Environmental Values,* 22(2), pp.191–215.

Ellen MacArthur Foundation and McKinsey Centre for Business and Environment. 2015. *Growth Within: A Circular Economy Vision for a Competitive Europe.* https://ellenmacarthurfoundation.org/growth-within-a-circular-economy-vision-for-a-competitive-europe.

Ferguson, M.E. and Souza, G.C. 2010. *Closed-loop Supply Chains. New Developments to Improve the Sustainability of Business Practices.* CRC Press.

Friant, M.C., Vermeulen, W.J.V. and Salomone, R. 2020. A typology of circular economy discourses: navigating the diverse visions of a contested paradigm. *Resources, Conservation and Recycling,* 161, p.1004917. https://doi.org/10.1016/j.resconrec.2020.104917.

Frosch, R.A. and Gallopoulos, N.E. 1989. Strategies for manufacturing. *Scientific American,* 261, pp.144–152. https://doi.org/10.1038/scientificamerican0989-144.

Geissdoerfer, M., Savaget, P., Bocken, N.M.P. and Hultink, E.J. 2017. The circular economy – a new sustainability paradigm? *Journal of Cleaner Production,* 143, pp.757–768. https://doi.org/10.1016/j.jclepro.2016.12.048.

Genovese, A. and Pansera, M. 2019. The circular economy at a crossroad: technocratic eco-modernism or convivial technology for social revolution? *Capitalism Nature Socialism,* 32(2), pp.95–113. https://doi.org/10.1080/10455752.2020.1763414.

Ghisellini, P., Cialani, C. and Ulgiati, S. 2016. A review on circular economy: the expected transition to a balanced interplay of environmental and economic systems. *Journal of Cleaner Production,* 114, pp.11–32. https://doi.org/10.1016/j.jclepro.2015.09.007.

Greenwood, L., Nash, T. and Whitehead, E. 2018. *Transforming our Economy: Financing the Social Enterprise Sector in Aotearoa New Zealand.* The Impact Initiative. www.theimpactinitiative.org.nz/publications/transforming-our-economy.

Gregson, N., Crang, M., Fuller, S. and Holms, H. 2015. Interrogating the circular economy: the moral economy of resource recovery in the EU. *Economy and Society*, 44(2), pp.218–243. https://doi.org/10.1080/03085147.2015.1013353.

Greyson, J. 2007. An economic instrument for zero waste, economic growth and sustainability. *Journal of Cleaner Production*, 15(13, 14), pp.1382–1390. https://doi.org/10.1016/j.jclepro.2006.07.019.

Hickel, J. and Kallis, G. 2020. Is green growth possible? *New Political Economy*, 25(4), pp.469–486. https://doi.org/10.1080/13563467.2019.1598964.

Holden, E., Linnerud, K. and Banister, D. 2017. The imperatives of sustainable development. *Sustainable Development*, 25(3), pp.213–226. https://doi.org/10.1002/sd.1647.

ICSU and ISSC. 2015. *Review of Targets for the Sustainable Development Goals: The Science Perspective*. International Council for Science.

Institute of Cetacean Research. 2007. *Whales as Food and Japanese Culture*. www.icrwhale.org/eng/59FoodCulture.pdf.

IRP (International Resource Panel). 2017. *Assessing Global Resource Use: A Systems Approach to Resource Efficiency and Pollution Reduction*. [Bringezu, S., Ramaswami, A., Schandl, H., O'Brien, M., et al.] A report of the International Resource Panel. Nairobi: United Nations Environment Programme.

Jackson, T. 2016. *Prosperity without Growth: Foundations for the Economy of Tomorrow*, 2nd ed. Routledge.

Kallis, G. 2011. In defence of degrowth. *Ecological Economics*, 70(5), pp.873–880. https://doi.org/10.1016/j.ecolecon.2010.12.007.

Kaza, S., Yao, L., Bhada-Tata, P. and Van Woerden, F. 2018. *What a Waste 2.0. A Global Snapshot of Solid Waste Management to 2050*. International Bank for Reconstruction and Development/The World Bank.

Kim, R.E. 2016. The nexus between international law and the sustainable development goals. *Review of European, Comparative and International Environmental Law*, 25(1), pp.15–26. https://doi.org/10.1111/reel.12148.

Kirchherr J., Reike, D. and Hekkert, M. 2017. Conceptualizing the circular economy: an analysis of 114 definitions. *Resources, Conservation and Recycling*, 127, pp.221–232. https://doi.org/10.1016/j.resconrec.2017.09.005.

Korhonen, J., Nuur, C., Feldmann, A. and Birkie, S.E. 2018. Circular economy as an essentially contested concept. *Journal of Cleaner Production*, 175, pp.544–552. https://doi.org/10.1016/j.jclepro.2017.12.111.

Kotzé, L.J. and Adelman, S. 2022. Environmental law and the unsustainability of sustainable development: A tale of disenchantment and of hope. *Law Critique*. https://doi.org/10.1007/s10978-022-09323-4.

Kovacic, Z., Strand, R. and Völker, T. 2019. *The Circular Economy in Europe: Critical Perspectives on Policies and Imaginaries*. Routledge.

Kunzig, R. 2020. Let's not waste this crucial moment: we need to stop abusing the planet. *National Geographic*. www.nationalgeographic.com/magazine/article/lets-not-waste-this-crucial-moment-we-need-to-stop-abusing-the-planet-feature.

Lacy, P. and Rutqvist, J. 2015. *Waste to Wealth*. Palgrave MacMillan. https://doi.org/10.1057/9781137530707.

Lewandowski, M. 2016. Designing the business models for circular economy – towards the conceptual framework. *Sustainability*, 8(1), 43. https://doi.org/10.3390/su8010043.

Liu, Q., Li, H., Zuo, X., Zhang, F. and Wang, L. 2009. A survey and analysis on public awareness and performance for promoting circular economy in China: a case study from Tianjin. *Journal of Cleaner Production*, 17(2), pp.265–270. https://doi.org/10.1016/j.jclepro.2008.06.003.

Liu, Z., Adams, M. and Walker, T.R. 2018. Are exports of recyclables from developed to developing countries waste pollution transfer or part of the global circular economy? *Resources, Conservation and Recycling*, 136, pp.22–23. https://doi.org/10.1016/j.resconrec.2018.04.005.

Mathews, J.A. and Tan, H. 2016. Circular economy: lessons from China. *Nature*, 531, pp.440–442. https://doi.org/10.1038/531440a.

McDonough, W. and Braungart, M. 2002. *Cradle to Cradle: Remaking the Way we Make Things*. North Point Press.

Millar, N., McLaughlin, E. and Börger, T. 2019. The circular economy: swings and roundabouts? *Ecological Economics*, 158, pp.11–19. https://doi.org/10.1016/j.ecolecon.2018.12.012.

Moktadir, Md.A., Rahman, T., Rahman, Md.H., Ali, S.M. and Paul, S.K. 2018. Drivers to sustainable manufacturing practices and circular economy: a perspective of leather industries in Bangladesh. *Journal of Cleaner Production*, 174, pp.1366–1380. https://doi.org/10.1016/j.jclepro.2017.11.063.

Murray, A., Skene, K. and Haynes, K. 2017. The circular economy: an interdisciplinary exploration of the concept and application in a global context. *Journal of Business Ethics*, 140, pp.369–380. https://doi.org/0.1007/s10551-015-2693-2.

OECD. 2018. *Global Material Resources Outlook to 2060: Economic Drivers and Environmental Consequences*. www.oecd.org/environment/waste/highlights-global-material-resources-outlook-to-2060.pdf.

Parrique, T., Barth, J., Briens, F., Kerschner, C., Kraus-Polk, A., Kuokkanen, A. and H Spangenberg, J. 2019. *Decoupling Debunked: Evidence and Arguments against Green Growth as a Sole Strategy for Sustainability*. European Environmental Bureau. https://eeb.org/library/decoupling-debunked/.

Peddle, M.T. 1990. Industrial Park location: do firm characteristics matter? *Journal of Regional Analysis & Policy*, 20(2), 26–36. https://doi.org/10.22004/ag.econ.129021/.

Raworth, K., 2017. A doughnut for the anthropocene: humanity's compass in the 21st century. *The Lancet Planetary Health*, 1(2), pp.e48–e49. https://doi.org/10.1016/S2542-5196(17)30028-1.

Robinson, S.A. and Carlson, D.A. 2021. A just alternative to litigation: applying restorative justice to climate-related loss and damage. *Third World Quarterly*, 42(6), pp.1384–1395. https://doi.org/10.1080/01436597.2021.1877128.

Rodriguez-Anton, J.M., Rubio-Andrada, L., Celemín-Pedroche, S. and Alonso-Almeida, M.D.M. 2019. Analysis of the relations between circular economy and sustainable development goals. *International Journal of Sustainable Development and World Ecology*, 26(8), pp.708–720. https://doi.org/10.1080/13504509.2019.1666754.

Ross, A. 2009. Modern interpretations of sustainable development. *Journal of Law and Society*, 36(1), pp.32–54.

Schroeder P, Anggraeni, K. and Weber, U. 2019. The relevance of circular economy practices to the sustainable development goals. *Journal of Industrial Ecology*, 23(1), pp.77–95. https://doi.org/10.1111/jiec.12732.

Scotford, E. 2007. Trash or treasure: policy tensions in EC waste regulation. *Journal of Environmental Law*, 19(3), pp.367–388. https://doi.org/10.1093/jel/eqm022.

Soma, T. 2016. The tale of the crying rice: the role of unpaid foodwork and learning in food waste prevention and reduction in Indonesian households. In: Sumner, J. (Ed.), *Learning, Food, and Sustainability*. Palgrave Macmillan. https://doi.org/10.1057/978-1-137-53904-5_2.

Stahel, W.R. and Reday, G. 1976. *The Potential for Substituting Manpower for Energy*. A report to the Commission of the European Communities, Brussels.

Steenmans, K. 2018. *Enabling Industrial Symbiosis through Regulations, Policies and Property Rights*. PhD Thesis. University of Surrey, UK.

Steenmans, K. and Malcolm, R. 2020. Transitioning towards circular systems: property rights in waste. *Journal of Property, Planning and Environmental Law*, 12(3), pp.219–234. https://doi.org/10.1108/JPPEL-03-2020-0018.

Steffen, W., Richardson, K., Röckstrom, J., Cornell, S.E., Fetzer, I., Bennett, E.M., Biggs, R., Carpenter, S.R., De Vries, W., De Wit, C.A., Folke, C., Gerten, D., Heinke, J., Mace, G.M., Persson, L.M., Ramanathan, V.R., Reyers, B. and Sörlin, S. 2015. Planetary boundaries: guiding human development on a changing planet. *Science*, 347(6223), p.1259855. https://doi.org/10.1126/science.1259855.

UNEP and ISWA. 2015. *Global Waste Management Outlook*. United Nations Environment Programme. Wilson, D.C. et al. https://www.unep.org/resources/report/global-waste-management-outlook.

United Nations. 2015. *Transforming Our World: The 2030 Agenda for Sustainable Development*. https://sdgs.un.org/2030agenda.

Vattenfall. 2022. *Waste – Transforming Waste to Energy*. https://group.vattenfall.com/what-we-do/our-energy-sources/waste.

Velenturf, A.P.M., Purnell, P., Macaskie, L.E., Mayes, W.M. and Sarpsford, D.J. 2020. A new perspective on a global circular economy. In: Macaskie, L.E., Sapsford, D.J. and Mayes, W.M. (Eds.), *Resource Recovery from Wastes: Towards a Circular Economy*, pp.1–22. Croydon: Royal Society of Chemistry.

Weiss, E.B. 1990. Our rights and obligations to future generations for the environment. *American Journal of International Law*, 84(1), pp.198–207.

Wiedmann, T., Lenzen, M., Keysser, L.T. and Steinberger, J.K. 2020. Scientists' warning on affluence. *Nature Communications*, 11, p.3107. https://doi.org/10.1038/s41467-020-16941-y.

Wolloch, N. 2017. *Nature in the History of Economic Thought: How Natural Resources became an Economic Concept*. Routledge.

Yuan, Z., Bi, J. and Moriguichi, Y. 2006. The circular economy: a new development strategy in China. *Journal of Industrial Ecology*, 10(1–2), pp.4–8. https://doi.org/10.1162/108819806775545321.

2 Locating Circular Economies within the Law

Understanding the status quo of the legal landscape helps reveal dominant understanding of circular economy (CE) practices, limitations of current implementations, and opportunities for future generations of laws facilitating just and inclusive CEs. This chapter reviews three ways in which the CE is governed by law: through explicitly labelled CE laws, laws underpinning CE principles, and laws impacting CEs. Predominantly national, but also subnational and supranational, laws are used to exemplify how laws are designed to support and enable CE transitions.

2.1 Introduction

To date, the analysis of CEs within the legal landscape has been limited and fragmented due to the broad spectrum of governance levels, sectors, and stakeholders relevant to the CE concept. Scholarly investigations of CEs and the law tend to focus on particular mechanisms identified as conducive to enabling greater circularity (such as extended producer responsibility (EPR) or ecodesign), sector case studies (such as electric vehicles or plastics), or particular (supra) national examples. This chapter provides an overview and foundation for understanding CE and the law by reviewing legal areas and mechanisms supporting CEs and CE transitions broadly.

Due to its wide-ranging nature, CE and the law cannot be described as an exact concept. The challenge is therefore in constructing CE and the law in such a way that strikes a balance to ensure its focus is not too narrow so that it can achieve its sustainable development objective (see Section 1.3), while simultaneously ensuring it is not so broad as to render it meaningless. For this purpose, we demarcate between three categories of laws within the legal landscape to understand the current (lack of) balance: (1) laws explicitly labelled as CE laws, (2) laws

DOI: 10.4324/9780429355141-2

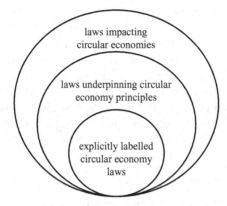

Figure 2.1 The concentric relationship between approaches to CE and the law.

embodying or implementing principles of the CE concept but not introduced as 'CE laws' per se, and (3) laws underpinning CE implementations. As illustrated in Figure 2.1, these categories are not distinct; for example, explicitly labelled CE laws can embody and implement principles of the CE, but not all of the latter categories will necessarily be found in an explicitly labelled CE law.

The remainder of this chapter reviews each category – Section 2.2 explicitly labelled CE laws, Section 2.3 laws embodying or implementing CE principles, and finally, Section 2.4 laws underpinning CEs – by drawing on supranational, national, and subnational laws.[1] Section 2.5 concludes by identifying strengths and weaknesses within the first generation of CE and the law, and proposes steps forward for the next generation.

2.2 Explicit Circular Economy Laws

Some laws adopted are explicitly labelled CE. These laws are significant, as labels can help activate concepts through fostering a forum and providing new opportunities for engagement with environmental issues (Hajer 1995; Lilja 2009). Most explicitly labelled CE laws are recent developments reflecting a growing traction of the concept. This section covers explicit CE laws adopted in Japan (2000), China (2008), Germany (2012),[2] Uruguay (2017), South Korea (2018), France (2020), and Mexico (2021). Even though in Japan and South Korea the explicit label of CE is not used, they are included nonetheless as they use words that are in essence synonymous with CEs (material-cycle and resources circulation, respectively – see Table 2.2).

Other explicit CE laws are currently being developed or going through the legislative enactment process. In Rwanda, for example, there is an intention to enact a legal framework for the CE (Ministry of Environment, Rwanda 2019, policy statement 2), whereas in Scotland, a Circular Economy Bill was proposed in 2019, then postponed in 2020 because of the coronavirus (SARS-CoV2) pandemic and is currently under consultation until end of August 2022 (Scottish Government 2022).

2.2.1 Circular Economy Definitions

Definitions of CE in explicitly labelled CE laws are set out in Table 2.1. These generally reflect areas of scholarly and practitioner definitional consensus (see Section 1.3) by centring around the environmental themes of: (1) prevention of wastes, and (2) reuse and recycling of wastes and resources within production and consumption processes. Only Mexico's General Circular Economy Law and Japan's Basic Act for Establishing a Sound-Material-Cycle Society cover additional dimensions. Mexico's General Circular Economy Law states that the CE is, in part, a system that maintains the value and use of products within the economy, whereas Japan's Basic Act for Establishing a Sound-Material-Cycle Society incorporates social dimensions in its definition for 'sound material-cycle society' (emphasis added), though there is inconsistency in that the Act's definition of 'cyclical use' does not.

Definitions in law delineate what is and is not covered by laws. When the dominant environmental focus of CE definitions in law limits meta-narratives to waste and resource efficiency, the result is that social issues are explicitly excluded. The absence of social dimensions is perhaps unsurprising given the ministerial stakeholders often involved in the CE law and policy-making processes. Weber and Stuchtey (2019) documented the ministerial stakeholders involved in CE law and policy development. The research found that only economy and environment ministerial stakeholders were involved in developing CE roadmaps across most EU countries, with Denmark the sole exception by involving the Ministry of Education (Weber and Stuchtey 2019). The lack of references to economic dimensions within the definitions is less problematic in our view. 'Economy' is included within the term itself and, beyond the linguistic focus, economic factors are the main motivators for – and barriers to – CE transitions (e.g., Galvão et al. 2018; Grafström and Aasma 2021).

Table 2.1 Definitions in explicitly labeled CE laws

CE law	Provision	CE definition
Japan's Basic Act for Establishing a Sound-Material-Cycle Society 2000	Art. 2(1), (3), and (4)	Sound-material-cycle society: a society in which the consumption of natural resources will be conserved and the environmental load will be reduced to the greatest extent possible, by preventing or reducing the generation of wastes, etc. from products, etc. by promoting proper cyclical use of products, etc. when these products, etc. have become circulative resources, and by ensuring proper disposal of circulative resources not put into cyclical use circulative resources: useful things among wastes, etc. cyclical use: reuse, reclamation, and heat recovery.
China's Circular Economy Promotion Law 2008	Art. 2	A generic term for the reducing, reusing, and recycling activities conducted in the process of production, circulation, and consumption.
Germany's Circular Economy Act 2012	S. 3(19)	The prevention and recovery of waste.
Uruguay's Sustainable Circular Economy Rules 2017	N/A	Not defined.[3]
South Korea's Framework Act on Resources Circulation 2018	Art. 2(1)	Resources circulation: utilising and managing the process of resources circulation in an environment-friendly manner to the extent necessary to accomplish the objectives of environmental policies, such as reducing the generation of wastes and appropriately recycling or treating … wastes generated.
France's Anti-Waste and Circular Economy Law 2020	N/A	The transition towards a circular economy aims *to achieve a neutral ecological footprint while complying with the framework of planetary boundaries* and to go beyond the linear economic model comprising extraction, manufacturing, consumption, and disposal by calling for economical and responsible consumption of natural resources and primary raw materials as well as, in order of priority, the prevention of waste, in particular through the reuse of products, and, in accordance with the waste treatment hierarchy, the reuse, recycling or, as a last resort, recovery of waste….[4]
Mexico's General Circular Economy Law 2021	Art. 3.VIII	System of production, distribution, and consumption of goods and services, orientated to the redesign and reincorporation of products and services to maintain the value and useful life of the products, materials, and resources associated with them as long as possible in the economy, and that the generation of waste is prevented or minimised, reincorporating it back into cyclical or biological production processes, in addition to promoting changes in production and consumption habits.[5]

CE: circular economy.

2.2.2 Overview of Measures

In line with the CE definitions in laws, environmental aims are central to the CE law objectives, particularly in relation to resource efficiency and consumption (see Table 2.2). Japan's Basic Act for Establishing a Sound-Material-Cycle Society is the only explicit CE law that does not refer to wastes or resources in its objective, though resources are covered by the definition of 'sound-material society', which is the Act's aim. In contrast to the definitions in law, and academic and practitioner discussions (see Section 1.3), social motivations feature more prominently than economic dimensions across the objectives, though still not consistently (health in Germany's Circular Economy Act, and Japan's Basic Act for Establishing a Sound-Material-Cycle Society, and a culture of environmental responsibility in Mexico's General Circular Economy Law, compared to economic development and activities only in the latter).

The weighting given to each of these dimensions is, however, not reflected within the remainder of the provisions. There are only perfunctory mentions of social dimensions in that the CE concept can support social development (Art. 3 of China's Circular Economy Promotion Law), as part of a culture of environmental responsibility (Art. 2.VII of Mexico's General Circular Economy Law), or that local governments take into account 'social conditions of their jurisdictions' when formulating and implementing policies for a transition to a resource-circulating society (Art. 5(2) of South Korea's Framework Act on Resources Circulation). The economic dimension is given much more weight by explicit CE laws mandating that CEs should be pursued where they are economically feasible and make economic sense (e.g., s.7(4) of Germany's Circular Economy Act and Art. 7 of Japan's Basic Act for Establishing a Sound-Material-Cycle Society).

Only half of CE laws (China's Circular Economy Promotion Law, South Korea's Framework Act on Resources Circulation, and Mexico's General Circular Economy Law) explicitly recognise sustainable development within their objectives (see Section 1.3). Mexico's General Circular Economy Law is a notable exception as some of its objectives closely align with some of the Sustainable Development Goals (SDGs) beyond the clear link to SDG 12 (responsible consumption and production): for example, Art 2.IX echoes the focus of SDG 11 (sustainable cities and communities); Art. 2.X aligns with SDG 7 (affordable and clean energy); and Art 2.III resonates with elements of SDG 9 (industry, innovation, and infrastructure). Moreover, Japan has implemented the only CE law to recognise intergenerational dimensions:

Table 2.2 Objectives of explicitly labelled CE laws

CE law	Provision	Objective
China's Circular Economy Promotion Law 2008	Art. 1	To develop the circular economy, improve resource efficiency, protect and improve the environment, and realise sustainable development.
Germany's Circular Economy Act 2012	S. 1(1)	To promote the circular economy in order to conserve natural resources and to ensure the protection of human health and the environment in the generation and management of waste.
Uruguay's Sustainable Circular Economy Rules 2017	N/A	Not included.[6]
South Korea's Framework Act on Resources Circulation 2018	Art. 1	To prescribe basic matters necessary for preserving the environment and creating a sustainable resource-circulating society, by reducing the generation of wastes to the maximum extent possible through the efficient use of resources and by decreasing the consumption of natural resources and energy through promoting circular utilisation and appropriate treatment of wastes generated.
France's Anti-Waste and Circular Economy Law 2020	Art. 1	This law amends the French Environment Code. The Code includes the objective of sustainable development, which includes the commitment to a circular economy (article 110-1.III). It amends the principles of the Code including Article 110-1-2 of the Code: 'The purpose of the provisions of this code is, as a priority, the prevention of resource use, then the promotion of economical and responsible consumption of resources *based on ecodesign*, then to ensure a hierarchy of the use of resources priorities resources from recycling or renewable sources, then recyclable resources, then other resources, while having consideration of the overall life cycle assessment' (amendment italicised).

(Continued)

CE law	Provision	Objective
Japan's Basic Act for Establishing a Sound-Material-Cycle Society	Art. 1	To promote comprehensively and systematically the policies for the establishment of a Sound-Material-Cycle Society and thereby help ensure healthy and cultured living for both the present and future generations of the nation, through articulating the basic principles on the establishment of a Sound-Material-Cycle Society, in conformity with the basic philosophy of the Environment Basic Act (Act No. 91 of 1993), clarifying the responsibilities of the state, local governments, business operators and citizens, and articulating fundamental matters for making policies for the formation of a Sound-Material-Cycle society including those for establishing the fundamental plan for Establishing a Sound-Material-Cycle Society.
Mexico's General Circular Economy Law	Art. 2	I Promote efficiency in the use of products, services, materials, energy, water, secondary raw materials, by-products through clean production, reuse, recycling, and redesign, or any circular economy criteria, as well as energy recovery to comply with Zero Waste policies; II Promote the observation of the Circular Economy Criteria in economic activities; III Facilitate technological development for recycling, reuse, and redesign of products, based on circular economy principles; IV Stimulate economic development through the promotion of actions that comply with circular economy principles; V Promote and encourage products to incorporate the Circular Economy Criteria; VI Promote the integration of value chains in relation to this Law; VII Promote and spread a culture of environmental co-responsibility in the population to achieve responsible consumption; VIII Complete the economic and environmental chains for resource flows; IX Facilitate the transformation towards sustainable cities and communities under sustainability criteria; X Promote the use, generation, and access to clean and renewable energy in accordance with Circular Economy principles; and XI Promote the transition towards a culture of greater sustainability.

CE: circular economy

the objective of the sound-material-cycle society is for the benefit of both current and future generations (Art. 1).

The inconsistent recognition and unequal representation of the three pillars of sustainable development is also reflected within explicitly labelled CE laws. In the laws, measures are primarily orientated towards environmental dimensions, and specifically towards wastes and resources. In some explicitly labelled CE laws, there is an additional disproportionate focus on particular waste operations. For example, Germany's Circular Economy Act 2012 transposes the EU's Waste Framework Directive's (2008/98/EC) waste hierarchy, which prioritises prevention. Yet, the prevention-reuse-recycling-recovery-disposal priority order is not mirrored in the substance of measures covered by the Act. The main prevention measure mandated is the establishment of waste prevention programmes (s. 33), whereas many more provisions cover recovery, such as obligation of waste producers or holders to recover waste (though exceptions apply) (s. 7); separate waste collection (s. 9); banning of certain wastes within products (s. 10(1)(1)); and waste management plans (s. 30). There are, however, some explicit CE laws that provide additional measures on waste prevention. Both France's Anti-Waste and Circular Economy Law and Japan's Basic Act for Establishing a Sound-Material-Cycle Society, for example, go beyond a plan by including provisions on repairability and durability to prevent waste generation (Art. 62 and Art. 20(i), respectively).

Current generations of explicitly labelled CE laws are also limited by the types of measures implemented. There is some variation, but also much repetition across the laws. The development of a CE strategy, plan, or programme, for example, is included in: China's Circular Economy Promotion Law 2008 (Art. 12); Uruguay's Sustainable Circular Economy Rules (Art. 2); South Korea's Framework Act on Resources Circulation (Art. 11); France's Anti-Waste and Circular Economy Law for single-use plastic packaging (Art. 7); Japan's Basic Act for Establishing a Sound-Material-Cycle Society (Art. 15); and Mexico's General Circular Economy Law (Art. 10.I).

There is a general recognition that various types of actors at different (governance) levels should be involved in the implementation of measures, though the particulars on the actors to be involved and how to involve them varies. South Korea's Framework Act on Resources Circulation, for example, places different stakeholders at the forefront of its CE law. Art. 3 of the Act states that the state, local governments, and all members of society (including business entities and citizens) must comply with basic principles of a resource-circulating society to minimise waste generation and use those wastes that are produced circularly, where such principles are economically and technically feasible. Japan's Basic Act for Establishing a Sound-Material-Cycle Society, however, does not explicitly state that various actors are central to the Act's CE principles, but recognises that there are roles for state, local governments, business operators, and citizens (Art. 4). The respective responsibilities of the actors range from formulating and implementing policies and measures, to conducting business activities in accordance with the basic principles of the cyclical use and disposal of circulative resources, to making efforts to reduce waste generation (Art. 9 to 12). The recognition and details are more limited in Germany's Circular Economy Act 2012 with the Federal Government the dominant focus. The German Federal Government is assigned powers and responsibilities in more than 20 provisions, whereas the *Land* Governments (the 16 partly sovereign states within Germany) are only assigned powers in two provisions. Civil society similarly has a very limited role with it only covered by public participation in the formulation of waste management plans (s. 32).

Even though a range of actors are identified to support CE implementations, there is a limited explicit recognition that actors across different sectors should be included to effect system-wide transitions from linear to CEs (see Chapter 3). This is both from the angle of waste generation (i.e., different sectors produce different wastes) and the services that different sectors can provide in supporting waste management (i.e., the role of research and education sectors compared to investment sectors in facilitating CEs). France's Anti-Waste and Circular Economy Law provides an example of a law that acknowledges both these angles. The Law links to a number of other non-environmental codes, including the Consumer Code in relation to information and spare parts of electronic and electrical equipment; the Education Code to raise awareness of reuse and waste reduction, and to teach students about ecodesign and respect of natural resource preservation; the Public Health Code regarding medical waste management; as well as amendments to the Public Property, Maritime, Highway, Insurance, Housing and Construction, and Regional and Local Authorities Codes. In contrast, Japan's Basic Act for Establishing a Sound-Material-Cycle Society has a narrower focus on waste management operations with links predominantly to laws on the recycling of particular types of waste (e.g., direct links are made to the Contained and Packaging Recycling Act; Small Home Appliance Recycling Act; Construction Recycling Act; End-of-life Vehicle Recycling Act).[7] Recognising legal areas beyond environmental law for enabling CEs (see Section 2.4) is likely to result in the integration of a wider range of actors.

2.2.3 Multilevel Circular Economy Laws

National-level laws and policies are only one piece of a much bigger CE and law puzzle. The EU's Circular Economy Action Plan (European Commission 2020a) is at the forefront of many CE discussions as the seminal supranational example. Much has been published, adopted, and proposed on the CE since its initial Circular Economy Package adopted in 2014[8] (e.g., Domenech and Bahn-Walkowiak 2019; European Commission 2020b; Friant et al. 2021; Johansson 2021).

Beyond CE laws at (supra)national level, there is also an emerging trend of explicitly labelled CE initiatives at community and federal level. For example, Castilla-La Mancha, an autonomous community holding legislative powers in Spain, implemented its Law 7/2019 on the Circular Economy on 29 November 2019 to incorporate CE principles within the region's legal system 'in order to promote economic growth, job creation and the generation of conditions that favour sustainable development ... with the consequent improvement of the environment and, therefore, of people's lives and well-being' (Art. 1). Some of the measures covered in Law 7/2019 to achieve this objective include implementing a CE strategy through councils and administrative bodies involved with water, energy, industry, economy, finance, commerce, consumption, education, land, and spatial planning (Art. 6(6)). In contrast to the national explicitly labelled CE laws, the mandated strategy has a dominant sectoral focus. The strategy should initially prioritise resource and waste production and consumption within the food, construction and demolition, industrial, and tourism sectors.

Moreover, cities are adopting explicitly labelled CE policies, such as Amsterdam Circular Strategy 2020–2025 (the Netherlands),[9] Circular Glasgow (UK),[10] Circular Peterborough (UK),[11] and London's Circular Economy Route Map (UK).[12] Other cities, such as Abuja Centenary City (Nigeria), Cape Town (South Africa), Curitiba (Brazil), Lavasa (India), Mumbai (India), and Maribor (Slovenia), have been identified by the Ellen MacArthur Foundation (EMF) as pioneering and legacy cities for incorporating CE principles, but have not used the explicit 'CE' label in naming their policies (Dhawan and Beckmann 2019). Initiatives by non-state actors, including city networks, aim to support transitions towards circular cities: C40 Cities Climate Leadership Group (C40) has a knowledge hub on CE and an 'Advancing Towards

Zero Waste Declaration' that cities can sign[13]; Circle Lab for Cities is implemented by Circle Economy, ICLEI – Local Governments for Sustainability, Metabolic, and EMF[14]; the EU's Circular Cities and Regions Initiative supports implementation of local and regional CEs across the EU's cities and regions[15]; and the EMF has set up a number of initiatives involving non-state actors, including the 'Circular Economy in Cities' which is 'a suite of online resources which provide a reference point for urban policymakers'.[16]

2.2.4 Summary

This section has shown that there is increasing adoption of explicitly labelled CE laws. The underlying critique of the current generation of such CE laws is that their meta-narratives are too narrowly construed by predominantly focusing on environmental dimensions of waste reuse, recycling, and other recovery, and often have an economic caveat that CEs should only be pursued where economically feasible or make economic sense. Even though waste prevention is acknowledged and sometimes identified as the priority, the substance of the laws is focused on waste management measures. There is also inconsistent recognition and unequal representation of economic, social, multi-sectoral, and multilevel dimensions of CE laws' design and impact.

2.3 Laws Underpinning Principles of Circular Economy

There are various ways through which laws can implement principles of CEs explicitly or implicitly. An explicitly labelled CE law or policy may mandate a law or policy to support CE aims, such as in the case of France's Anti-Waste and Circular Economy Law, which amends other existing national codes, or mandates by explicit CE laws to adopt CE plans, strategies, or programmes (see Section 2.2). Alternatively, laws may link to the CE itself. Such CE links are not necessarily established when a law is first implemented but may occur retrospectively. For example, the EU's Waste Framework Directive (2008/98/EC) includes the CE as part of its aim as a result of a 2018 amendment[17]; China's Law of the Prevention and Control of Environmental Pollution by Solid Waste 1995 was amended in 2004 to include CE[18]; and plastic bag bans in Rwanda were identified a decade after their initial implementation as conducive to the CE by the Rwandan government (Biruta 2019), but the laws themselves do not explicitly refer to CE.[19]

Even without a direct CE link established by an explicitly labelled CE law or within the law itself, laws can underpin principles of CEs through aligning with the CE concept's aim and central actions of prevention, reuse, recycling, and recovery of wastes and resources. China's Promotion of Cleaner Production Law 2002, for instance, aims

> to promote cleaner production, increase the efficiency of the utilisation rate of resources, reduce and avoid the generation of pollutants, protect and improve environments, ensure the health of human beings and promote the sustainable development of the economy and society.
>
> (Art. 1). This provision is similar to the objective stated in China's Circular Economy Promotion Law 2008 (see Table 2.2).

Moreover, the Promotion of Cleaner Production Law 2002 covers the use and recycling of waste throughout (e.g., Art. 20 covers life cycles of products and packaging), and the definition of cleaner production within the Law also has clear overlaps with the CE concept:

> the continuous application of measures for design improvement, utilisation of clean energy and raw materials, the implementation of advanced processes, technologies and equipment, improvement of management and comprehensive utilisation of resources to reduce pollution at source, enhance the rates of resource utilisation efficiency, reduce or avoid pollution generation and discharge in the course of production, provision of services and product use, so as to decrease harm to the health of human beings and the environment.
>
> (Art. 2)

Explicit links to CE are, however, not made within the law itself, though the links are recognised in scholarly literature (e.g., Zhu et al. 2019). Such approaches are also reflected in policies with Vietnam's National Strategy of Integrated Solid Waste Management up to 2025 identified as providing the regulatory framework for implementing the CE (e.g., Schneider et al. 2017), without explicitly using the term.

Laws underpinning CE principles are not limited to the national level. For instance, the Basel Convention on the Control of Transboundary Movements of Hazardous Wastes and Their Disposal (Basel Convention), obliges states to minimise the generation of hazardous and other wastes (Art. 4(2)(a)) and requires Parties to take appropriate measures to ensure the transboundary movement of hazardous wastes and other wastes only be allowed if ... (b) [t]he wastes in question are required as a raw material for recycling or recovery industries in the State of import.

(Art. 4(9))

The ways in which the Basel Convention currently underpins CE principles overall, however, is limited, but there is much scope for it to become a key instrument to directly facilitate (or hinder) global CEs (Hagen et al. 2021) (see Chapter 4 on circular plastic wastes).

In the remainder of this section, we provide examples of mechanisms that can be, and are being, adopted to promote the prevention, reuse, recycling, and recovery actions of the CE concept. No measure discussed below is sufficient on its own, but instead a portfolio of measures is needed to facilitate CE transitions (Milios 2018, 2021; Vence and Pérez 2021). Below we discuss both market-based and command-and-control measures, which may be either voluntary or mandatory (Milios 2018, 2021).

2.3.1 Market-Based Measures

Market-based measures that can facilitate CE transitions include charges, environmental taxation, and container deposit schemes. Charges (e.g., plastic bag charges) aim to incentivise a producer or consumer behavioural change by increasing the price of products or raising revenues for the purpose of specific (environmental) uses or for general use (Kandelaars 1999). In contrast to charges, which are payments for which a service is given in return, a tax (e.g., landfill tax) is added to the government budget without a direct service in return (Kandelaars 1999). In container deposit schemes, consumers are charged a deposit when purchasing goods in certain containers (e.g., bottle, can), which is reimbursed when the container is returned. Such schemes are already well-established in a number of countries.[20]

Each of these market-based measures has their own benefits and issues. For instance, landfill and incineration taxes can reduce environmental effects with a low economic impact (Freire-González et al. 2022). Freire-González et al. (2022) demonstrated that gross domestic product (GDP) was only reduced by 0.045 percent in a stimulation of high tax rates without using tax revenues to subsidise recycling in Spain (Freire-González et al. 2022). Taxes on their own, however, do not necessarily reduce overall consumption of materials and may give rise to equity and justice issues (Walker et al. 2020). Taxes can have both regressive and distributional impacts (see Chapter 3). Wier et al.'s (2005) case study on carbon dioxide (CO_2) taxes on energy consumption in households in Denmark demonstrated that households with lower incomes pay a greater share of their resources than those with higher incomes. Moreover, there are intergenerational distributional implications, as older generations alive at the time the pollution taxes are introduced may suffer welfare losses on account of the intergenerational redistribution in favour of generations yet to be born (Bovenberg and Heijdra 1998). Environmental taxation does not have to be inherently regressive and there are three ways in which concerns of regressivity can be addressed: (1) exempt some amount of consumption of the taxed item (e.g., pollution, energy use, water use) from the environmental tax; (2) use revenues to reduce an existing tax that is as regressive or more regressive than the new environmental tax; and (3) use revenues to reduce an existing tax in a way that increases the progressivity of that tax (Hammond et al. 1999).

Beyond existing examples of market-based measures in laws underpinning CE principles, they are also directly advocated for in certain explicitly labelled CE laws. For instance, the EU's Circular Economy Action Plan encourages 'the broader application of well-designed economic instruments', such as environmental taxation (e.g., landfill and incineration tax), and the use of value-added tax (VAT) rates (European Commission 2020a); Uruguay's Sustainable Circular Economy Rules provide for the option to implement financial incentives, such as tariff benefits related to CE activities (Art. 6); and Mexico's General Circular Economy Law includes measures for the development of tax incentives to promote CE (Chapter 6 – Art.–22–25). The latter, Mexico's General Circular Economy Law, has been accused, however, for being in part motivated by bringing the informal recycling sector (see Section 4.3.1) under the tax system rather than environmental benefits (Espinoza 2022).

As highlighted above by the justice issues of taxation, market-based measures impacts require investigation both in relation to the ways in which they can be implemented and their effectiveness. Moreover, the effectiveness of market-based measures needs examination before implementation, as they do not always result in the anticipated outcomes. Milios (2021), for example, reviewed Swedish VAT reduction in repair services and found that even though there had been an increased frequency of tax repairs, the repairs could not be linked to the tax change.

2.3.2 *Command-and-Control Measures*

Non-market-based measures to incentivise CEs include administrative (e.g., bans, standards, targets) and informative (e.g., labels, certifications, information campaigns) command-and-control instruments (Milios 2021). Similar to market-based measures, command-and-control measures are used within both explicitly labelled CE laws and laws underpinning CE principles.

Targets adopted in relation to waste management often focus on reducing quantities going to landfill or incineration while increasing the amount of waste being recycled. This is the case in the EU, where such targets dominate CE measures. There is much scope to extend targets beyond the common focus of waste management operations to the design of products by, for example, setting targets of amounts of recyclable material to use in the production of a product.

Targets may be supported by bans or bans may be a standalone measure. A ban is commonly adopted to prevent certain wastes and resources, such as bans on imports of certain wastes (e.g., Kojima 2020) and plastic bag bans (see Nielsen et al. 2019). Challenges of such measures include banned items and processes being replaced by alternatives with similar or other (unintended) consequences. For example, while China's import ban on certain plastic and other wastes implemented by Operation National Sword in 2017 resulted in almost halving the trade flow of global plastic waste, it also resulted in a redirecting and accumulation of wastes in neighbouring countries such as Malaysia and Vietnam who did not have the best available recycling operations in place to manage the imports (Wang et al. 2020; Wen et al. 2021). Plastic bag bans are similarly not solely eco-beneficial. The Danish Government conducted a life cycle assessment that concluded that paper bags are not necessarily better for the environment than plastic bags (Ministry of Environment and Food of Denmark 2018). Using certain environmental indicators,[21] simple plastic bags should be reused at least one time for grocery shopping bags and can be directly used as waste bin bags to minimise climate change impacts, whereas organic and conventional cotton bags must be reused at least 149 and 52 times, respectively, and at least 20,000 and 7100 times considering all indicators, and unbleached paper bags reused at least 43 times (Ministry of Environment and Food of Denmark 2018). There is thus a need to consider the impact of legal mechanisms on the complete life cycles of products, the purpose of products, and whether products would be replaced.

Many of the laws and policies implemented recently to focus on the environmental impacts of products include EPR (Gupt and Sahay 2015). EPR entails shifting responsibility for waste management from consumers and authorities, the traditional assignees, to the producer of the products. Different types of responsibility can be assigned: physical responsibility, economic responsibility, liability, and informative responsibility (Lindhqvist 2000). Physical responsibility is where the producer is involved in physical management of the products and/or their development, production, and marketing of products that can be re-used, are technically durable and suitable for safe and high-quality recovery, and environmentally compatible disposable. Ways in which physical responsibility can be implemented includes through the use of ownership regimes (e.g., leasing goods like clothes, producer retaining ownership of the packaging in which a product such as soap is contained). Economic responsibility is where a producer covers all or part of the costs for managing the wastes at the end of a product's life, for example, for the collection, processing, and disposal of materials. Where there is economic responsibility, EPR can be described as a market-based measure as it relies on market incentives (Sachs 2006). Liability is where responsibility for environmental damages caused by a product is borne by its producer. This may encompass damages occurring at various stages in the life cycle, including use and final disposal. Finally, informative responsibility is where the producer is required to provide information on the product (e.g., labelling) and its impacts at various life cycle stages. Forms of EPR are included in explicitly labelled CE laws. Germany's Circular Economy Act 2012, for example, has a provision on physical responsibility in terms of the development and production of products: those

> who develop, manufacture, process, treat or sell products shall bear product responsibility with regard to the achievement of the objectives of circular economy. Products must be so designed, if at all possible, that waste generation within their production and use is reduced, and that environmentally compatible recovery and disposal of the waste resulting from their use is ensured.
>
> (s. 23(1))

There are many issues with the current implementation of EPR schemes. Research has highlighted that often EPR focuses on end-of-life rather than delivering ecodesign changes and allocating sufficient responsibility to producers, challenges of producer responsibility organisations that are often used to implement EPR, and a lack of transparency of some EPR schemes (e.g., Kunz et al. 2018; Campbell-Johnston et al. 2020). This has led to calls, such as those proposed by Maitre-Ekern (2021), to incorporate a 'pre-market producer responsibility' within legal frameworks to ensure that there is a focus on developing durable, repairable, and reusable products. Justice issues of EPR are discussed in Chapter 3 (see Section 3.4.1).

Instead of having the producer retain responsibility for dealing with waste of a product, right to repair laws intend to extend the product lifetimes. Right to repair laws are relatively recent developments. The right to repair is generally not defined in the laws and does not require producers to repair, but often means that producers should either provide information to facilitate repairs and/or provide accessibility to spare parts. Australia's Competition and Consumer Amendment (Motor Vehicle and Service and Repair Information Sharing Scheme) Act 2021, for example, applies to light good vehicles (less than 3.5 tonnes) manufactured on or after 1 January 2002 and passenger vehicles that have up to nine seating positions (including that of driver) manufactured on or after 1 January 2002. The Law obliges manufacturers to provide information for use in diagnosing faults with servicing or repairing covered vehicles. The current scope of existing right to repair laws is limited in the products on which they focus, with many not covering smartphones and laptops, which are often a key focus of obsolescence. France's right to repair law, Anti-Waste and Circular Economy Law 2020, is currently an exception, as it does cover electrical and electronic equipment. Unlike other laws though it does not require availability of spare parts, but instead is concerned with producers, importers, distributors, or other sellers providing a repairability index of equipment to inform the consumer about the ability to repair the product. From 1 January 2024, producers and importers in France will also have to provide a durability index free of charge (should include criteria such as reliability and robustness, and complement the repairability criteria).

Measures like producer responsibility and right to repair are in part aimed at incentivising product (eco)design. Product design schemes use incentives and do not necessarily have to be as a result of certain responsibility or right to repair, but may be a measure on its own. Within a CE context, such schemes could, for example, focus on preventing waste generated during production and consumption, as well as promote design aimed at preventing obsolescence in terms of the product itself and through enabling repair, and where not possible to facilitate recycling (or other recovery) of the product or its parts (see e.g., Van Doorsselaer 2022). Ecodesign is a particular product design approach within the EU that integrates 'environmental aspects into product design with the aim of improving the environmental performance of the product throughout its whole life cycle' (Ecodesign Directive 2009/125/EC, Art. 2(23)).[22]

Reporting requirements could therefore be implemented either to support other measures promoting CEs by incentivising compliance with such measures or to report on the circularity of a system to incentivise the implementation of other measures facilitating CE transitions. Mandatory food waste reporting, for example, is often suggested as an action to complement other food waste reduction mechanisms (e.g., WWF 2021). Reporting could stimulate the prevention of food waste, thereby supporting transition to a more sustainable CE. Few mandatory food waste laws exist: Japan's Food Recycling Law 2001 requires food-related businesses that generate food waste of more than 100 tonnes per year to report the amount of food waste generated pursuant to Art. 9, and South Korea's Wastes Control Act 2007 requires persons discharging 'large quantities of food wastes' to report to the competent local authority on their plans to restrain the generation of food wastes and properly treat such wastes (Art. 15-2). Even though reporting may be costly, there is evidence that environmental reporting may save money (Bebbington and Thy 1999). There are again limitations and challenges of reporting, including identifying metrics to measure circularity for reporting purposes, administrative capacity, and institutional capacity (e.g., Bebbington and Thy 1999; Gray 2006).

2.3.3 Summary

Laws can implement principles of CEs directly through a link in the law itself to CE or as a result of a mandate by an explicitly labelled CE law, or indirectly through promoting the CE concept's aim and central actions of prevention, reuse, recycling, and recovery of wastes and resources. This section has provided examples of both market-based (e.g., charges, taxation, container deposit schemes) and command-and-control (e.g., bans, labelling, producer responsibility, product design, reporting requirements, right to repair, standards, targets) measures that can be used to underpin the CE. None are sufficient to support a complete transition to a CE, with most also not distinct to the CE concept. The listed measures do not necessarily promote it, with examples even existing where the covered measures hinder CE transitions (e.g., fossil fuel subsidies). There is thus a danger of greenwashing with measures presented as conducive to CEs which are in actuality irrelevant or may act as a barrier.

2.4 Laws Impacting Circular Economies

The broad-ranging nature and impacts of CEs require more than the predominant environmental (particularly waste and resource) law focus currently provided by explicitly labelled CE laws and laws underpinning CE principles. If the scope of the current legal landscape of CE and the law is not widened, then there may be a similar outcome to the EU's waste hierarchy. The hierarchy's earlier interpretations had broad applicability, whereas current operationalisations have a much narrower focus on waste treatment activities rather than prevention at source. There is nascent recognition in scholarly literature that other areas of law should complement, support, and action CE objectives, but very limited research analysing these links.

Table 2.3 provides an overview of areas of law beyond environmental law identified in academic literature as having links to the CE concept. More granularity can be provided for some areas of law listed. One such example is how public procurement contracts have been a particular focus of the CE concept within contract law (e.g., Witjes and Lozano 2016; Alhola et al. 2019). In contrast, there is only initial recognition of a link with other areas of law (e.g., human rights law). Examples of particular questions within these areas of laws linked to the CE concept are listed in Table 2.3, but questions generally applicable to all areas include:

- What is the role of X law in promoting CEs?
- How can X law be designed to meet the needs of a CE?
- How can CE aims be taken into account when shaping X law?
- What are the incentives, opportunities, risks, barriers, and challenges?

Even though the legal areas discussed are presented as distinct, some areas overlap (e.g., private law encompasses, for example, contract law) and some questions transgress several areas of law, such as: what are the human rights implications of resource ownership within a CE? Some of the measures and mechanisms identified in Section 2.3 further demonstrate overlaps (see Figure 2.1): landfill tax is a mechanism often adopted as part of preceding category of laws underpinning principles of CE laws, but also falls within the area of tax law. A further commonality (and pre-empting discussion in Chapter 3) is that the justice angle has an important role in all areas of law and the transition to a CE.

Table 2.3 Non-exhaustive overview of questions identified or discussed in relation to the CE concept within areas of law beyond environmental law

Area of law	Question	Literature
Competition	How can competition law reinforce exemptions for environmentally beneficial coordination between businesses to create CE systems?	Benton and Hazell (2013)
Consumer	What is the role of consumer protection and consumer law in promoting CEs?	Backes (2017); Keirsbilck and Terryn (2019); Mak and Lujinović (2019); Micklitz (2019); Dalhammar (2020); Mak and Terryn (2020)
	How should consumer law be designed to meet the needs of a CE?	
	How can CE aims be taken into account when shaping consumer law?	
Contract	How are breach of contract rights (e.g., third-party repair rights in common law) affected as users instead as owners?	Van Kogelenberg (2018); De Boeck (2019); Beheshti (2020)
	What are the impacts of inequality in bargaining position, which result in adhesion contracts and unfair terms, within the context of contracts governing sharing products or servitisation?	
	How to operationalise the cancellation of the contract?	
Corporate	How can CE aims and principles be integrated into corporate social and environmental responsibility?	Thomas (2019)
Economic	What is the basis for a legal framework for the CE that can contribute to social and economic prosperity without threatening planetary boundaries?	Velenturf et al. (2020); Norouzi et al. (2022)
Financial law	How are CE transitions and implementations to be financed?	UNEP Finance Initiative (2020); Schröder and Raes (2021)
	What is the role of law and regulation in enabling the financing of CE transitions?	
	How to ensure legal readiness for CE finance?	
Human rights	What are the human rights implications as a result of the unsustainable levels of resource extraction and production, and waste production, and the resultant environmental issues?	Backes (2017); Velenturf et al. (2020); Mies and Gold (2021); Bianchini et al. (2022)

(*Continued*)

Area of law	Question	Literature
Intellectual property	What are the intellectual property implications of designing products for CEs?	Wiens (2014); Thomas (2019); Ballardini et al. (2021)
	How to overcome the intellectual property rights to CEs in relation to inhibiting the sharing of information and innovation between businesses and manufacturers?	
	How to overcome barriers of intellectual property rights limiting possibilities to repair goods protected by intellectual property?	
Private	How can private law provide the incentives needed for directing innovations and businesses towards CE models in relation to specific issues related to, e.g., repairing, reusing, and leasing?	Backes (2017); Thomas (2019); Ballardini et al. (2021)
Property	How can we promote a better balance between private property and societal interest within private law in order to promote CEs?	Ploeger et al. (2019); Steenmans et al. (2020); Thomas (2020); Ballardini et al. (2021)
	How can private law provide the incentives needed for directing innovations and businesses towards CE models in relation to specific issues related to, e.g., repairing, reusing, and leasing?	
Tax	What is the role of tax measures (e.g., tax exemption) in promoting CEs?	Ellen MacArthur Foundation (2015); Li and Lin (2016); Backes (2017)

The level of detail varies significantly across the literature – for example, Steenmans et al. (2020) is a Special Issue dedicated to exploring property rights dimensions of CEs, whereas Backes (2017) and Velenturf et al. (2020) only acknowledge the existing links between CE and consumer, private, and human rights law.
CE: circular economy.

The integration of other areas of law impacting CEs is likely to become more evident and explicit in subsequent generations of CE and the law, as needs are identified and the concept permeates more sectors and areas. For example, as with many transitions, access to finance is a commonly cited barrier that needs to be overcome for facilitating CE transitions (e.g., Stucki et al. 2019; Grafström and Aasma 2021). Some mechanisms already exist and include legal measures on public financing, such as the National Fund for Circular Economy set out in Uruguay's Sustainable Circular Economy Rules (Art. 9), as well as private financial mechanisms, such as CE-themed green bonds and green loans (e.g., Intesa Sanpaolo 2019), but more development is expected in this area as the reality of implementing transitions takes hold.

Linking CE to, and with, other legal domains more clearly will require a delicate balance. Future generation CE laws will need to encompass other legal domains while still ensuring its usefulness and meaningfulness as law.

2.5 Conclusion

There is no clearly bounded area of CE and the law, but instead it comprises a broad spectrum of generalist and specialist mechanisms. We have demarcated three categories of laws: CE laws, laws underpinning CE principles, and laws impacting CEs. There is at present a lack of balance between these three categories. Laws and policies promoting CEs generally fall within the second category, whereas only a few explicitly labelled CE laws have been implemented and there is often only an emerging recognition of the need to integrate the CE concept into other areas of law. Environmental law, especially resource and waste law, tends to dominate the current generation of laws underpinning CE principles and explicitly labelled CE laws. Across the three categories of CE and the law, the concept transgresses governance levels and sectors, and involves a range of actors, which adds to a diffuse legal landscape. CE's legal landscape is further complicated by narratives and interlinkages across the different categories not always clearly joining up, for example, through not consistently recognising justice issues or limiting the legal discourse of the environmental law.

The risk of the broad spectrum of governance levels, sectors, and stakeholders relevant to the CE concept is the need to ensure CE and the law remains a useful and meaningful area. If too widespread, then law risks fuzziness, vagueness, and ambiguity. Yet, at the same time, the variation in CE and the law is not causing the systemic shift towards CEs needed to address current critical resource and waste crises. We therefore propose bringing justice into the frame in Chapter 3 in order to address some of the critical limitations and challenges of the legal framing of the concept currently.

Notes

1 There is bias in the examples provided, as the identification of case studies was limited by our language knowledge.
2 Initially, the Closed Cycle and Waste Management Act (*Kreislaufwirtschafts- und Abfallgesetz*) was adopted in Germany in 1996. Even though the literal translation is the Circular Economy and Waste Act, it was not referred to as such, likely because its initial approach was limited and focused on efficient collection of packaging waste and plastics recycling schemes (Schulz et al. 2019). The Act was revised in 2012 and resulted in the adoption of the Circular Economy Act (*Kreislaufwirtschaftsgesetz*) (i.e., the literal translation is now commonly accepted). The motivation and linguistic reasons for change in translation are beyond the scope of this book.
3 In the motivation statement following the rules, the CE is defined as the reincorporation of waste into production processes following repair and/or recycling.
4 France's Anti-Waste and Circular Economy Law amends Article 110-1-1 of the Code, which does not explicitly introduce a definition of the CE per se, but has the following effect:

> The transition towards a circular economy aims *to achieve a neutral ecological footprint while complying with the framework of planetary boundaries* and to go beyond the linear economic model comprising extraction, manufacturing, consumption, and disposal by calling for economical and responsible consumption of natural resources and primary raw materials as well as, in order of priority, the prevention of waste, in particular through the reuse of products, and, in accordance with the waste treatment hierarchy, the reuse, recycling or, as a last resort, recovery of waste. ...
>
> (amendment italicised).

5 Authors' unofficial translation, as the Law is currently only available in Spanish on government websites.
6 The Rules set out a statement of motivation. This includes the high volume of wastes produced and the economic opportunities of circular approaches for employment, social inclusion, and sustainable economic development.
7 There are a few links to acts that do not refer to recycling, but these are still focused on waste management operations rather than sectors more widely: Waste Management Act; Act on the Promotion of Effective Utilization of Resource; Act on Special Measures against Industrial Waste; Act on Special Measures concerning Promotion of Proper Treatment of PCV Wastes; and Act on Promotion of Procurement of Eco-Friendly Goods and Services by the State and Other Entities.
8 This was withdrawn in December 2014, with the 2015 Circular Economy Action Plan launched in 2015 (European Commission 2015).
9 See www.amsterdam.nl/en/policy/sustainability/circular-economy.

10 See www.circularglasgow.com. See also Circle Economy and Chamber of Commerce (2022).
11 See www.futurepeterborough.com/circular-city.
12 See https://relondon.gov.uk.
13 See www.c40knowledgehub.org/s/topic/0TO1Q000000011h0WAA/circular-economy?language=en_US (knowledge hub on CE) and www.c40.org/other/zero-waste-declaration (zero waste declaration that cities can sign).
14 See https://circulars.iclei.org/circle-lab-for-cities/.
15 See https://circular-cities-and-regions.eu.
16 See www.ellenmacarthurfoundation.org/our-work/activities/circular-economy-in-cities.
17 Waste Framework Directive, Art. 1: 'This Directive lays down measures to protect the environment and human health by preventing or reducing the generation of waste, the adverse impacts of the generation and management of waste and by reducing overall impacts of resource use and improving the efficiency of such use, which are crucial for the transition to a circular economy and for guaranteeing the Union's long-term competitiveness'. The inclusion of CE is as a result of Directive (EU) 2018/851 of the European Parliament and of the Council of 30 May 2018 amending Directive 2008/98/EC [2018] OJ L 150/109.
18 China's Law of the Prevention and Control of Environmental Pollution by Solid Waste 1995: 'The state shall promote green development methods and facilitate the development of cleaner production and circular economy' (Art. 3).
19 Plastic bags were first banned in 2008 as a result of Law No 57/2008 of 10/09/2008 relating to the prohibition of manufacturing, importation, use, and sale of polythene bags in Rwanda. This law has since been repealed and replaced to extend the ban to single-use plastics (Law No 17/2019 of 10/08/2019 relating to the prohibition of manufacturing, importation, use, and sale of plastic carry bags and single-use plastic items).
20 Bottle Bill Resource Guide by the Container Recycling Institute provides an overview of current and proposed laws globally: www.bottlebill.org.
21 Environmental indicators used by the Ministry of Environment and Food of Denmark (2018) study: ozone depletion, human toxicity, terrestrial acidification, terrestrial eutrophication, water resource depletion, and resource depletion.
22 Directive 2009/125/EC of the European Parliament and of the Council of 21 October 2009 establishing a framework for the setting of ecodesign requirements for energy-related products (recast) [2009] OJ L285/10.

References

Alhola, K., Ryding, S.-O., Salmenperä, H. and Busch, N.J. 2019. Exploiting the potential of public procurement: opportunities for circular economy. *Journal of Industrial Ecology,* 23(1), pp.96–109. https://doi.org/10.1111/jiec.12770.

Backes, C. 2017. *Law for a Circular Economy.* The Hague: Eleven International Publishing.

Ballardini, R.M., Kaisto, J. and Similä, J. 2021. Developing novel property concepts in private law to foster the circular economy. *Journal of Cleaner Production*, 279, p.123747. https://doi.org/10.1016/j.jclepro.2020.123747.

Bebbington, J. and Thy, C. 1999. Compulsory environmental reporting in Denmark: an evaluation. *Social and Environmental Accountability Journal*, 19(2), pp.2–4, https://doi.org/10.1080/0969160X.1999.9651612.

Beheshti, R. 2020. The circular economy and the implied terms of contract in English sales law. *Journal of Property, Planning and Environmental Law*, 13(1), pp.31–45. https://doi.org/10.1108/JPPEL-09-2020-0042.

Benton, D. and Hazell, J. 2013. *Resource Resilient UK: A Report from the Circular Economy Task Force*. Green Alliance. https://green-alliance.org.uk/wp-content/uploads/2021/11/Resource-resilient-UK.pdf.

Bianchini, A., Guarnieri, P. and Rossi, J. 2022. A framework to assess social indicators in a circular economy perspective. *Sustainability*, 14(13), p.7970. https://doi.org/10.3390/su14137970.

Biruta, V. 2019. *Remarks by Minister Biruta at 2019 National Circular Economy Forum*. http://fonerwa.org/blog/remarks-minister-biruta-2019-national-circular-economy-forum.

Bovenberg, L. and Heijdra, B.J. 1998. Environmental tax policy and intergenerational distribution. *Journal of Public Economics*, 67(1), pp.1–24. https://doi.org/10.1016/S0047-2727(97)00064-9.

Campbell-Johnston, K., Friant, M.C., Thapa, K., Lakerveld, D. and Vermeulen, W.J.V. 2020. How circular is your tyre: experiences with extended producer responsibility from a circular economy perspective. *Journal of Cleaner Production*, 270, p.122042. https://doi.org/10.1016/j.jclepro.2020.122042.

Circle Economy and Glasgow Chamber of Commerce. 2022. *Circular Economy, Enabling the Transition towards Net-zero: how Glasgow Businesses can Embrace the Circular Economy to keep the World under 1.5 Degrees of Warming*. www.circularglasgow.com/wp-content/uploads/2022/01/20220128-Glasgow-Net-Zero-1.pdf.

Dalhammar, C. 2020. Sustainability, the circular economy and consumer law in Sweden. *Journal of European Consumer and Market Law*, 9(3), pp.125–128.

De Boeck, A. *The Rise of the Sharing Economy versus Contract Law: challenges and Questions*. http://www.iuscommune.eu/html/activities/2019/2019-11-28/workshop_13b_De_Boeck.pdf.

Dhawan, P. and Beckmann, J. 2019. Circular economy guidebook for cities. CCSP. https://circulareconomy.europa.eu/platform/en/toolkits-guidelines/circular-economy-guidebook-cities.

Domenech, T. and Bahn-Walkowiak, B. 2019. Transition towards a resource efficient circular economy in Europe: policy lessons from the EU and the Member States. *Ecological Economics*, 155, pp.7–19. https://doi.org/10.1016/j.ecolecon.2017.11.001.

Ellen MacArthur Foundation and McKinsey Centre for Business and Environment. 2015. *Growth Within: A Circular Economy Vision for a*

Competitive Europe. https://ellenmacarthurfoundation.org/growth-within-a-circular-economy-vision-for-a-competitive-europe.

Espinoza, S.G. 2022. *Noticias. Secretaria del Medio Ambiente.* www.sadsma. cdmx.gob.mx:9000/circular/blog/post/economia-circular-por-ley.

European Commission. 2015. *Closing the Loop - An EU Action Plan for the Circular Economy (Communication).* COM (2015) 614 final.

European Commission. 2020a. *A New Circular Economy Action Plan. For a Cleaner and More Competitive Europe (Communication).* COM(2020) 98 final.

European Commission. 2020b. *Annex to the Circular Economy Action Plan* (Communication). COM(2020) 98 final.

Freire-Gonzalález, J., Martinez-Sanchez, V. and Puig-Ventosa, I. 2022. Tools for a circular economy: assessing waste taxation in a CGE multi-pollutant framework. *Waste Management,* 139, pp.50–59. https://doi.org/10.1016/j. wasman.2021.12.016.

Friant, M.C., Vermeulen, W.J.V. and Salomone, R. 2021. Analysing European Union circular economy policies: words versus actions. *Sustainable Production and Consumption,* 27, pp.337–353. https://doi.org/10.1016/j.spc.2020.11.001.

Galvão, G.D.A., de Nadae, J., Clemente, D.H., Chinen, G. and de Carvalho, M.M. 2018. Circular economy: overview of barriers. *Procedia CIRP,* 73, pp.79–85. https://doi.org/10.1016/j.procir.2018.04.011.

Grafström, J. and Aasma, S. 2021. Breaking circular economy barriers. *Journal of Cleaner Production,* 292, p.126002. https://doi.org/10.1016/j. jclepro.2021.126002.

Gray, R. 2006. Does sustainability reporting improve corporate behaviour? Wrong question? Right time? *Accounting and Business Research,* 36(1), pp.65–88. https://doi.org/10.1080/00014788.2006.9730048.

Gupt, Y. and Sahay, S. 2015. Review of extended producer responsibility: a case study approach. *Waste Management & Research: The Journal for a Sustainable Circular Economy.* https://doi.org/10.1177/0734242X15592275.

Hagen, P., LaMotte, R. and Meng, D. 2021. The circular economy runs through Basel. *The Environmental Forum.* www.bdlaw.com/content/uploads/2021/08/ SeptOct2021_The-Environmental-Forum_LeadFeature.pdf.

Hajer, M.A. 1995. *The Politics of Environmental Discourse: Ecological Modernization and the Policy Process.* Clarendon Press.

Hammond, J., Merriman, H. and Wolff, G. 1999. Equity and distribution issues in the design of environmental tax reform. *Redefining Progress: Incentives Program.* http://citeseerx.ist.psu.edu/viewdoc/download?doi= 10.1.1.153.1868&rep=rep1&type=pdf.

Intesa Sanpaolo. 2019. *Intesa Sanpaolo Successfully Completes the Placement of the First Sustainability Bond Dedicated to the Circular Economy.* https://group.intesasanpaolo.com/en/newsroom/press-releases/2019/11/ sustainability-bond-en.

Johansson, N. 2021. Does the EU's Action Plan for a Circular Economy challenge the linear economy? *Environmental Science and Technology,* 55(22), pp.15001–15003. https://doi.org/10.1021/acs.est.1c06194.

Kandelaars, P. 1999. *Economic Models of Material-product Chains for Environmental Policy Analysis.* Kluwer Academic Publishers.

Keirsbilck, B. and Terryn, E. 2019. *Consumer Protection in a Circular Economy.* Intersentia Ltd.

Kojima, M. 2020. The impact of recyclable waste trade restrictions on producer recycling activities. *IJAT,* 14(6), pp.873–881. https://doi.org/10.20965/ijat.2020.p0873.

Kunz, N., Mayers, K. and Van Wassenhove, L.N. 2018. Stakeholder views on extended producer responsibility and the circular economy. *California Management Review,* 60(3), pp.45–70. https://doi.org/10.1177/0008125617752694.

Li, W. and Lin, W. 2016. Circular economy policies in China. In: Anbumozhi, V. and Kim, J. (Eds.), *Towards a Circular Economy: Corporate Management and Policy Pathways.* ERIA.

Lilja, R. 2009. From waste prevention to promotion of material efficiency: change of discourse in the waste policy of Finland. *Journal of Cleaner Production,* 17(2), pp.129–136. https://doi.org/10.1016/j.jclepro.2008.03.010.

Lindhqvist, T. 2000. *Extended Producer Responsibility in Systems.* PhD thesis. Lund University, Sweden.

Maitre-Ekern, E. 2021. Re-thinking producer responsibility for a sustainable circular economy from extended producer responsibility to pre-market producer responsibility. *Journal of Cleaner Production,* 286, p.125454. https://doi.org/10.1016/j.jclepro.2020.125454.

Mak, V. and Lujinović, E. 2019. Towards a circular economy in EU consumer markets: legal possibilities and legal challenges and the Dutch example. *Journal of European Consumer and Market Law,* 8(1), pp.4–12.

Mak, V. and Terryn, E. 2020. Circular economy and consumer protection: the consumer as a citizen and the limits of empowerment through consumer law. *Journal of Consumer Policy,* 43, pp.227–248. https://doi.org/10.1007/s10603-019-09435-y.

Micklitz, H.-W. 2019. Squaring the circle? Reconciling consumer law and the circular economy. *Journal of European Consumer and Market Law,* 8(6), pp.229–237.

Mies, A. and Gold, S. 2021. Mapping the social dimension of the circular economy. *Journal of Cleaner Production,* 321, p.128960. https://doi.org/10.1016/j.jclepro.2021.128960.

Milios, L. 2018. Advancing to a circular economy: three essential ingredients for a comprehensive policy mix. *Sustainability Transitions, Management, and Governance,* 13, pp.861–878. https://doi.org/10.1007/s11625-017-0502-9.

Milios, L. 2021 Towards a circular economy taxation framework: expectations and challenges of implementation. *Circular Economy and Sustainability,* 1, pp.477–498. https://doi.org/10.1007/s43615-020-00002-z.

Ministry of Environment and Food of Denmark. 2018. *Life Cycle Assessment of Grocery Carrier Bags.* Environmental Project no. 1985. Accessed 18 January

2021. https://www2.mst.dk/udgiv/publications/2018/02/978-87-93614-73-4. pdf.

Ministry of Environment, Rwanda. 2019. *National Environment and Climate Change Policy. June 2019.* www.fonerwa.org/sites/default/files/2021-06/Rwanda%20National%20Environment%20and%20Climate%20 Change%20Policy%202019.pdf.

Nielsen, T.D., Holmberg, K. and Stripple, J. 2019. Need a bag? A review of public policies on plastic carrier bags – where, how and to what effect? *Waste Management,* 87, pp.428–440. https://doi.org/10.1016/j.wasman. 2019.02.025.

Norouzi, N. 2022. A practical and analytic view on legal framework of circular economics as one of the recent economic law insights: a comparative legal Study. *Circular Economy and Sustainability.* https://doi.org/10.1007/ s43615-022-00147-z.

Ploeger, H., Prins, M., Straub, A. and van den Brink, R. 2019. Circular economy and real estate: the legal (im)possibilities of operational lease. *Facilities,* 37(9/10), pp.653–668. https://doi.org/10.1108/F-01-2018-0006.

Sachs, N. 2006. Planning the funeral at the birth: extended producer responsibility in the European Union and the United States. *Harvard Environmental Law Review,* 30, p.51.

Schneider, P., Anh, L.H., Wagner, J., Reichenbach, J. and Hebner, A. 2017. Solid waste management in Ho Chi Minh City, Vietnam: Moving towards a circular economy? *Sustainability,* 9(2), p.286. https://doi.org/10.3390/ su9020286.

Schröder, P. and Raes, J. 2021. *Financing an Inclusive Circular Economy: De-risking Investments for Circular Business Models and the SDGs.* Research Paper. Environment and Society Programme. Chatham House. https:// www.chathamhouse.org/sites/default/files/2021-07/2021-07-16-inclusive-circular-economy-schroder-raes_0.pdf.

Schulz, C., Hjaltadóttir, R.E. and Hild, P. 2019. Practising circles: studying institutional change and circular economy practices. *Journal of Cleaner Production,* 237, p.117749. https://doi.org/10.1016/j.jclepro.2019.117749.

Scottish Government. 2022. *Delivering Scotland's Circular Economy. A Consultation on Proposals for a Circular Economy Bill.* www.gov.scot/publications/delivering-scotlands-circular-economy-consultation-proposals-circular-economy-bill/documents/.

Steenmans, K., Malcolm, R. and Clarke, A. (Eds.) 2020. Special Issue: Rethinking property approaches in resources for the circular economy. *Journal of Property, Planning and Environmental Law,* 12(3), pp.185–186.

Stucki J, Flammini A, van Beers D, Phuong TT, Tram Anh N, Dong TD, Huy VQ, Hieu VTM. 2019. Eco-Industrial Park (EIP) development in Viet Nam: results and key insights from UNIDO's EIP Project (2014–2019). *Sustainability,* 11(17), p.4667. https://doi.org/10.3390/su11174667.

Thomas, S. 2019. Law and the circular economy. *Journal of Business Law,* 1, pp.62–83.

Thomas, S, 2020. Legal considerations for a circular economy. In: Tudor, T, and Dutra, C. (Eds.), *The Routledge Handbook of Waste, Resources and the Circular Economy*. Routledge.

UNEP Finance Initiative. 2020. *Financing Circularity: Demystifying Finance for Circular Economies*. www.unepfi.org/publications/general-publications/financing-circularity.

Van Doorsselaer, K. 2022. The role of ecodesign in the circular economy. In: Stefanakis, A. and Nikolaou, I. (Eds.), *Circular Economy and Sustainability*. Elsevier. https://doi.org/10.1016/B978-0-12-819817-9.00018-1.

Van Kogelenberg, M. 2018. Exploring the concept of servitisation on the intersection between property and contract law. *Ius Commune Conference 2018. Workshop Contract Law and Consumer Protection. Circular Economy and Servitisation*. 30 November 2018.

Velenturf, A.P.M., Purnell, P., Macaskie, L.E., Mayes, W.M. and Sarpsford, D.J. 2020. A new perspective on a global circular economy. In: Macaskie, L.E., Sapsford, D.J. and Mayes, W.M. (Eds.), *Resource Recovery from Wastes: Towards a Circular Economy*, pp.1–22. Royal Society of Chemistry.

Vence, X. and Pérez, S.J.L. 2021. Taxation for a circular economy: New instruments, reforms, and architectural changes in the fiscal system. *Sustainability*, 13(8), p.4581. https://doi.org/10.3390/su13084581.

Walker, T., Gramlich, D. and Dumont-Bergeron, A. 2020. The case for a plastic tax: a review of its benefits and disadvantages within a circular economy. In: Wasieleski, D.M. and Weber, J. (Eds.), *Sustainability (Business and Society 360, Vol. 4)*. Emerald Publishing Limited, pp.185–211. https://doi.org/10.1108/S2514-175920200000004010.

Wang, C., Zhao, L., Kim, M.K., Chen, W.-Q. and Sutherland, J.W. 2020. Structure of the global waste trade network and the impact of China's import ban. *Resources, Conservation and Recycling*, 153, p.104591. https://doi.org/10.1016/j.resconrec.2019.104591.

Weber, T. and Stuchtey, M (Ed.). 2019. *Pathways towards a German Circular Economy – Lessons from European Strategies*. National Academy of Science and Engineering.

Wen, Z., Xie, Y., Chen, M. and Dinga, C.D. 2021. China's plastic import ban increases prospects of environmental impact mitigation of plastic waste trade flow worldwide. *Nature Communications*, 12, p.425. https://doi.org/10.1038/s41467-020-20741-9.

Wiens, K. 2014. Intellectual property is putting circular economy in jeopardy. *The Guardian*. 4 June 2014. www.theguardian.com/sustainable-business/intellectual-property-circular-economy-bmw-apple.

Wier, M., Birr-Pedersen, K., Jacobsen, H.K. and Klok, J. 2005. Are CO_2 taxes regressive? Evidence from the Danish experience. *Ecological Economics*, 52(2), pp.239–251. https://doi.org/10.1016/j.ecolecon.2004.08.005.

Witjes, S. and Lozano, R. 2016. Towards a more circular economy: proposing a framework linking sustainable public procurement and sustainable business models. *Resources, Conservation and Recycling,* 112, pp.37–44. https://doi.org/10.1016/j.resconrec.2016.04.015.

WWF. 2021. *Driven to Waste: The Global Impact of Food Loss and Waste on Farms.* https://wwfint.awsassets.panda.org/downloads/wwf_uk__driven_to_waste___the_global_impact_of_food_loss_and_waste_on_farms.pdf.

Zhu, J., Fan, C., Shi, H. and Shi, L. 2019. Efforts for a circular economy in China: a comprehensive review of policies, *Journal of Industrial Ecology,* 23(1), pp.110–118. https://doi.org/10.1111/jiec.12754.

3 Equity, Justice, and Law in Circular Economies

In this chapter, we go beyond the review provided in Chapter 2 of circular economy (CE) laws. This chapter explores how worldviews and values embedded within a legal system have a determining influence on the social justice impacts that laws have when enacted, for instance, by excluding certain communities from access to resources or prioritising a growth-orientated economics. Exploring worldviews and values within the dominant legal systems can help to reveal the potential ways in which a CE as currently constructed could, if scaled up, result in perverse outcomes, exacerbating existing distributional, recognition, and procedural injustices.

3.1 Introduction

The CE is morphing 'from an early iteration that began with an emphasis on reduce, reuse, and recycle to one more ... that places greater emphasis on maximising the value from resources' (Reike et al. 2018). There is no single future CE. It can still take many different directions (Blomsma and Brennan 2017; Friant et al. 2020). Like other meta-normative concepts such as the free market and sustainable development, the concept belies complexities, not only technological but also political, economic, legal, social, and cultural. As such the CE is open to multiple interpretations by numerous actors who have different political, economic, and ideological values and interests. Any CE will become a reality through the actions of actors, networks, organisations, and states engaged in enterprise, policy, and law-making. Future CEs around the world will differ significantly depending on the value sets that underpin the laws, regulations, and policy design choices (Bauwens et al. 2020). This reality, however, is yet to be extensively reflected in law and policy research, nor have the

DOI: 10.4324/9780429355141-3

potential impacts, both socio-economic and ecological, that laws to promote a CE, will have.

The CE is coming of age as global challenges urgently need to be addressed. Collective action is necessary to address transnational challenges including climate change, biodiversity loss, post-coronavirus (SARS-CoV2) pandemic socio-economic recovery as well as the digital revolution. Collective action is increasingly problematised by geopolitical tensions between superpowers such as China, Europe, India, Russia, and the United States. To date, CE-related law's evolution has been largely ad-hoc at national and supranational levels. Laws adopted to achieve aspects of a CE are currently fragmented intersecting with established legal fields such as waste law, trade law, investment law, human rights law, as well as indigenous peoples' rights law and emerging nature law. There is no clear cross-cutting systemic approach (see Chapter 2).

Any future CE will require a fundamental systemic change to the foundations of the dominant linear economy. The extent and form of the changes required to fully achieve a CE are yet to be comprehensively researched. All too frequently the systemic shift to a CE is portrayed as a simple win-win-win for all within economy, society, and the environment (Genovese and Pansera 2021). Preston et al. (2019) warn that 'entrepreneurial optimism behind articulations of the CE ...will lead to an inevitable transition that ... will be superficial and tokenistic ultimately failing to deliver in terms of systemic change'. The CE is not a simple neutral concept that will equally benefit everyone; it is a political one over which there is a great deal of contestation. As such the laws and regulations adopted to transform the dominant linear economic system into a CE will result in winners and losers. Winners and losers are determined by both the processes to make laws, regulations, and standards adopted, both public and private, their substance, and the governance structures underpinning their implementation. CE legal frameworks could result in unsustainable circular lock-ins for countries leading to rebound effects whereby primary consumption continues to rise amongst the richest in society as the world's poor fall further behind in their share of wealth (Zink and Geyer 2017; Circle Economy 2022).

Laws to achieve a CE currently draw on the legal toolkit created by and employed within the linear economy globally: property, contract, tort, administrative, human rights, trade, and environmental. As illustrated in Chapter 2, current CE initiatives have yet to fully utilise existing legal tools to mobilise a systemic transition away from the current dominant linear economic model. Yet, we argue that such a project to design a systemic legal model using existing legal tools will not automatically deliver a fair and just CE. Indeed, a CE could further legally enclose resources, for example, though (intellectual) property rights and contract law, exacerbating existing elite actors' economic privileges, such as multinational enterprises, at the expense of already poor, vulnerable, and marginalised peoples (Thomas 2019a; Beheshti 2020; Perzanowski 2022).

There are multiple questions that need to be asked by researchers about the origins and purpose of the legal systems (civil and common) and their tools which form the backbone of the current linear economic system. Failing to examine the underlying historical and contemporary values that have shaped the dominant legal economic culture, a culture that perpetuates inequity, exclusion, and precarity especially for the majority of peoples in the Global South and indigenous peoples in the settled colonies (Latin America, North Americas, and Pacific regions) will be a serious omission if a sustainable, fair, and just CE is to be established.

In this chapter, we explore justice issues relating to law and CEs. We argue that research on justice by critical legal scholars and political ecologists, especially recent studies on environmental and climate change justice, are a valuable resource for scholars on how to interrogate the consequences of different law and policy approaches to creating CEs. In Section 3.2, we set out current legal research limitations on CE issues, and why justice issues need to be added to the agenda. Section 3.3 then outlines current material distributive inequities, as well as the legal roots underpinning injustices. In the final Section 3.4 drawing on justice scholarship, especially environmental and climate change, we take stock of distributive, recognition, and procedural justice issues that need to be in the frame when designing laws and policies to enable a just and inclusive CE.

3.2 Legal Research: A Limited Agenda

Legal research has paid limited attention to social justice dimensions of a CE transition. Similarly, consideration of the forms and structures any new CE might take and how these may, for example, impact those peoples whose livelihoods rely on informal economies has been off the radar of law and policy scholars (Carenzo et al. 2022). If CE legal research is to understand the interconnections between different areas of law and the impacts these can have, it needs to adopt a more systemic approach. Even CE advocates recognise a broader approach is necessary. Ekins et al. (2019) argued that 'though the circular economy provides a strong foundation, it is increasingly clear that we cannot continue to frame our relationship with the world solely through the lens of production and resource use. A fully circular transition also takes strides toward social goals'. For instance, the focus on technical standards and private law dimensions of 'closing the loop' has failed to consider the wider equity implications that measures may have (Thomas 2020b). This is particularly the case when it comes to wealth flows and value chains within global trade.

As Chapter 2 showed, most CE laws are national in focus. Trade and the CE, despite immense value of material flows across supply chains globally, is again only just becoming a research focus for governments, international organisations, and academics alike (Yamaguchi 2018; Barrie and Schröder 2021). The 2021 EU-UK Trade and Cooperation Agreement was the first EU Free Trade Agreement that explicitly referenced the CE (Art. 400(5.a)). However, the importance of getting social justice issues included onto CE trade research is imperative if a transition is to deliver a resilient sustainable global economic order. For example, a shift to circularity for the EU apparel industry is associated with 50,000 job opportunities in Europe; however, this would be matched by an estimated decline of over 400,000 jobs in value chains outside the region (Repp et al. 2021). In a 2022 report, it was noted that 'most sustainability policies driven by actors in high-income countries fail to balance their local concerns with global ones, exacerbating the divide between high and lower-income countries'. The report went on to warn that 'if actions aren't taken now to ensure a socially-just transition the world faces increased livelihood insecurity, and increased migration and displacement of people from lower-income countries; illegal and fraudulent trade; less resilient and secure supply chains [and potentially] civil unrest and instability' (Circle Economy 2022).

Despite environmental law driving many CE-related laws, we argue that at its core CE is the domain of economic legal research. As Frerichs (2013), a socio-legal scholar, argues all economic-related laws have 'positive, negative, variable, and unknown implications at every level of social life – on our actions and interactions, on the regimes by which we govern and are governed, and on the rationalities that guide us'. Thomas (2019b) observes that 'the legal consequences of moves to circular economy, the questions that might arise dealing with new forms of relationships and new socio-economic practices, never appear to have received consideration'. Geng et al. (2019) have noted that in academic scholarship real-world factors of a CE at scale are rarely considered, such as the implications of servitisation on employment, informal economies, and fiscal mechanisms such as extended producer responsibility (EPR). Meanwhile, Mavropoulos and Nilsen (2020) argue that CE law and policy research has 'ignore[ed] a well-established fact, that environmental, economic, and social problems are interwoven ... [and] as a consequence, each and every intervention in resource management, and especially worldwide intervention related with global supply chains, will result in very specific social and economic impacts'. The Tearfund, a Christian not for profit charity, has argued that the design and implementation of eco-design laws and policies in Europe will 'determine the success or failure of the circular economy in Low Income Countries' (Williams et al. 2018). Not only does the Tearfund recognise the interconnections between economic and environmental law impacts but also the extra-territorial reach of European law to the Global South. The current state of play of academic legal research and its limited focus is increasingly problematic considering the expanding commercial interest in the potential economic opportunities afforded by the CE. To avoid repeating patterns that are embedded within the linear economic system, legal scholars need to identify the role that law has played, and continues to do so, in creating inequity and injustice in the world today.

3.3 Economic Inequities

In this section, we outline current distributional material inequity before examining the role law has played historically in creating the situation globally today. The following section will then take stock of justice dimensions of law and the CE.

3.3.1 Global Material Distributional (In)equity

Since the industrial economic expansion, the Earth's ecological resources have been unsustainably consumed, fuelled by fossil fuels, labour, and ever-increasing volumes of cheap credit (Webster 2017). Elhacham et al. (2020) calculated that human-made mass, referred to as 'anthropogenic mass', was now equal to the mass of all living organisms on Earth. The research concluded that 'the accumulation of anthropogenic mass [had] reached 30 Gt per year, based on the average for the past 5 years [and that] this corresponds to each person on the globe producing more than his or her body weight in anthropogenic mass every week' (Elhacham et al. 2020). Elhacham et al.'s research, although useful in highlighting the scale of manufactured 'anthropocentric mass' on the planet, fails to recognise that the distribution of both harms and benefits within the modern extractivist economy are unequal amongst peoples and states in the world. Webster (2017) argues that both the flow of energy and wealth from natural resource extraction was made possible by a legal infrastructure designed to maximise consumption but not equitably.

Under the current linear economic system, there is gross material and wealth inequity globally. The global economy's material use has tripled over the past four decades (Oberle et al. 2019). However, there are significant differences in the material footprint between regions of the world. The annual per capita material footprint for the Asia-Pacific, Latin America and the Caribbean, and West Asia is between nine and ten tonnes, or half that of Europe and North America, which is about 20–25 tonnes per person. In contrast, Africa has an average material footprint of below three tonnes per capita (Oberle et al. 2019). Although these figures reveal the distributional inequity between regions globally in material consumption, it is the richest people in the world that have the greatest environmental footprint. The richest ten percent of the global population, comprising about 630 million people out of a world population of 7.8 billion (the majority are Europeans and North Americans) were responsible for about 52 percent of global emissions from 1990 to 2015 (Hardoon and Slater 2015). The divergence between the rich and everyone else is anticipated to only worsen as the global population increases. Based on historical research, the economist Piketty (2015) argues that if current trends continue, the richest one percent of the world's population will control a larger share of the world's wealth by 2030 than the remaining 99 percent.

Distributional inequality resulting from wealth flows has an ongoing inverse impact when it comes to environmental degradation and access to a healthy environment. Poverty is itself intertwined with the economy's externalities as much as its environmental impacts (Schröder et al. 2020). In 2022, the UN Special Rapporteur on Human Rights and the Environment David Boyd identified what he called 'sacrifice zones', where environmental degradation was at the greatest levels, around the world. Boyd observed that 'clusters of the most heavily polluting and hazardous facilities, such as open-pit mines, smelters, petroleum refineries, chemical plants and garbage dumps tend to be located near disadvantaged communities' (UN Human Rights Council 2022). Such 'sacrifice zones' confirms previous evidence of the disproportionate siting of waste facilities in areas where deprived and/or ethnic minorities are concentrated (Reams and Templet 1996; Martuzzi et al. 2010). The 'slow violence' from polluted air, water, soil, and degraded ecosystems is a legacy of accumulated environmental injustice over centuries (Nixon 2011). Explanations for these inequities include political powerlessness; economic vulnerability; cheap rents for investors to site polluting operators amongst poor and minority communities; and differential enforcement of environmental law (Reams and Templet 1996). Research into why people remained in 'sacrifice zones' found that there were economic imperatives, such as affordable housing and an inability to secure employment in areas believed to be safer (Reams and Templet 1996).

The next section turns to examine the legal roots of contemporary material and wealth inequality and related injustices.

3.3.2 Historical Roots of Environmental and Social Injustices

Environmental and social injustices have deep and extensive roots. There is nothing inevitable about the inequitable distribution of burdens of pollution, access to natural resources, and benefits from their consumption and wealth within any economy (Kojola and Pellow 2021). Laws, regulations, and standards, directly and indirectly, have a determining influence over who the winners and losers are in any economic system (Perrone and Schneidermann 2019). Those with the power and privilege in a system ultimately determine the rules in which their own ideological values are prioritised (Mattei and Nader 2008; Scherer et al. 2018; Pistor 2019). Values play out in ways that shape all areas relating to environmental and social justice issues. This is a fact that will apply to any future CE as much as it has played out within the linear economy.

The distributional inequity of wealth and benefits in the current global linear economic system has its roots in imperial and settler colonialism (Chibber 2014; Whyte 2018). A dominant Western rule of law approach contributed to and enforced a multilevel system that favoured the 'haves' over the 'have nots' using property, contract, administrative, and criminal laws (Mattei and Nader 2008). Enclosure and appropriation of resources, both material and human (slavery), were the legal foundations for the linear economic model (Patnaik and Patnaik 2021). The colonial encounter devastated the indigenous civilisations of Africa, the Americas, and Asia, and enabled European settlers to appropriate and exploit their lands, labour, and natural resources (Whyte 2018). Land clearances for extractivist industries such as mining, oil, and diamonds as well as agro-industrial monoculture plantations and National Parks have killed and continually led to displacement of peoples in colonised and settler countries since the 17th century (Ghosh 2021). Colonialism using law and violence converted what were previously self-reliant circular subsistence economies into outposts of Europe that exported low market value agricultural products, minerals, and timber, and imported high market value manufactured goods from colonising countries (Anghie 2005; Natarajan and Khoday 2014).

Since the mid-20th century, with the decline in territorial colonialism, the dominant international economic legal order based on the concept of free trade created an unequal playing field, which benefitted the developed countries at the expense of former colonies (Miles 2010; Chimni 2013). The terms of trade established under international law through the General Agreement on Trade and Tariffs in 1947 has consistently favoured manufactured goods, where value is added, over primary low value raw materials (Baars 2019). Transplanted legal templates resulted in former colonial states being caught up in a vicious cycle trying to use laws to develop economies to be like those of their former colonisers (Eslava 2015). For example, modern investment law inherited from the colonial era an instrumentalist view of the environment as an object of exploitation, with no corresponding duty to protect the health of local ecosystems, enhance the well-being of local communities, or advance the goals and interests of the host state (Miles 2010).

Confronted with an international economic order that privileged international financial institutions and developed countries, former colonial countries in the Global South often became tied into a debt spiral as they tried to pursue Modernist development ideals (de Sousa Santos 2002; Eslava 2015). Efforts to mitigate debt burdens resulted in desperate drives to attract foreign investment. Transnational corporations, mainly from the Global North, took advantage of lower environmental and labour standards in host countries. Investments compounded and added to existing social and environmental injustices because extractivist externalities were primarily shouldered by local under privileged populations in 'sacrifice zones' (Gonzalez 2001; Miles 2010). Given the historical background to global economic law, it is unsurprising that ecological debt and social injustice are at the heart of many North–South conflicts in international environmental and economic, especially trade and investment, laws (Mickelson 2005). Countries in the Global South continue to argue that the Global North owes an ecological debt for the 'resource plundering, unfair trade, environmental damage and the free occupation of environmental space to deposit waste' to address long-standing colonial injustices (Paredis 2009; Warlenius 2016).

Southern countries have demanded that the North assume responsibility for its immense contribution to major environmental problems, such as climate change. Since the 1950s the Global South has sought to mitigate the economic legacy of colonialism by calling for special and differentiated treatment in international economic law and common but differentiated responsibility in international environmental law (Rajamani 2006; Cullet 2016). In relation to climate change, the Global North has only accepted the principle of common but differentiated responsibility based on its superior technical and financial resources while repeatedly disavowing responsibility on the basis of its historic contributions to global crises (Gonzalez 2015). The reticence to assume responsibility by the Global North is particularly evident in negotiations over liability and compensation relating to loss and damage for small island and developing states, especially for low-lying coastal areas, from climate change impacts (Pekkarinen et al. 2019; Robinson and Carlson 2021). Failing to address these long-standing social inequities could become a threat multiplier to conflicts such as civil wars, displacement, and famine.

3.3.3 Summary

The environmental injustice legacies due to colonialism and the post-colonial legal order are the legal foundations upon which a CE is being constructed. Currently, legal research has not added to its agenda questions about how the justice legacies of past and current legal systems should be addressed in law and the CE. This section has demonstrated how integral it is for legal research on the CE to understand how current injustices were created and how they are perpetuated by law. It is also necessary to reframe CE-related law and policy research to incorporate equity and justice dimensions. In the next section, we turn to focus on three justice dimensions: distributional, recognition, and procedural. We first consider how selected CE-related laws may impact distributional justice before discussing recognition and procedural justice dimensions.

3.4 Justice Issues: Taking Stock

CE is in its infancy and yet to reach the scales predicted by its leading advocates. The role law will play in enabling the transition is yet to be fully determined. As Chapter 2 demonstrated, however, certain legal interventions, including EPR, (intellectual) property laws, and contract, are already preferred tools used to increase circularity in an economy. Whichever legal tools are employed to advance a CE, they will impact existing justice issues now and in the future. In this section, we take stock of existing CE-related laws justice issues and potential implications for the law in the future. We use Schlosberg's (2004) environmental justice tripartite approach: distribution, recognition, and procedural as the framework for our analysis. We will identify interconnections CE-related laws could have with distributive, recognition, and procedural justice depending on both their design and implementation. Given the nascent nature of CE and law, this is a hypothetical exercise rather than evidence-based drawing on environmental justice scholarship and selected case study research literature. The objective is to raise questions and issues of concern for current and future law and policy researchers working on transitioning to a CE.

3.4.1 Distributive Justice

Distributive justice is concerned with the allocation (distribution) of material goods and rights/duties, including benefits and burdens among members of a society. Its classic form is Rawls' veil of ignorance, in which if those who elaborate the rules of a society were to not know beforehand what their social position is, they would almost certainly desire a more equal society in which all members help each other share equal burdens and privileges (Kaswan 2021). All regulatory instruments and policies have consequences for distributive justice (Amorim de Oliveira 2021). The regulatory instruments and policies to promote a transition to a CE will not be an exception to this phenomenon. The harms and benefits from flows of materials and wealth will be distributed, both within current and future generations, dependent upon the CE's normative framing within related laws and policies. Given the potential consequences for current and future society, it is necessary for actors involved in advancing circularity to identify the distributive justice impacts those regulatory instruments and policies could have. In this section, we focus on one regulatory mechanism, EPR, which has its roots in waste law (see Chapter 2), to explore the potential distributive justice impacts a particular application and interpretation could result in.

CE advocates view EPR's promissory potential to unlock business opportunities to valorise material flows within an increasingly closed-loop, zero-waste economic system. By 2016, there were already 400 EPR schemes in use globally (OECD 2016). EPR is based upon the polluter-pays principle. The premise for EPR regulation is that the producer of a product will retain responsibility for the product throughout its useful life and at its end of useful life. Responsibility for the EPR regulation's distributive justice impacts are not those of the producer. As such we argue that EPR's potential distributive justice impacts need greater attention from all stakeholders, especially governments, as it is incorporated into more economic sectors, from the local to the global level.

Two areas of concern we discuss relating to potential EPR distributive justice dimensions, although by no means not the only ones, are first impacts on informal economy workers and, second, the consequences of increased commodification and enclosure of the global material commons.

First, the informal economy, where economic activity falls outside the regulated economy, employs, 61 percent of all workers, which is approximately two billion people worldwide (ILO 2018). The regions with the highest share of informality between 2010 and 2017 were sub-Saharan Africa, Latin America, and the Caribbean—both at 34 percent of gross domestic product (GDP) (Thomas 2019b). Globally agriculture and industry sectors have the highest percentage of informal workers: nearly 94 percent and 57 percent, respectively (OECD 2019). EPR in the CE and the bioeconomy will have distributive justice impacts for both industrial and agricultural sectors by (en)closing material cycles and establishing formalised, regulated business opportunities.

EPR can create commercial opportunities for business, especially those with the capital to invest in technologies. CE advocates argue that formalisation can deliver benefits for informal workers by providing secure, higher-skilled, better-paid employment which meets health and safety regulations, and ends precarity for millions (PACE 2017; UNIDO 2017; Chateau and Mavroeidi 2020). Yet research has shown that, for example, formalisation of the waste sector has often marginalised informal workers and made existence more precarious, especially for women and children (Woggsborg and Schröder 2018; Talbott 2022). In one instance, in Fortaleza, Brazil efforts to incorporate waste picker associations into new recycling systems had perverse outcomes. Waste picker associations found themselves at a disadvantage, even with government support, because there is 'often a minimum volume requirement by the [hi-tech] recycling companies that their capacity to collect, store, and process cannot fulfil' so they are unable to capitalise on the new income earning opportunities (Amorim de Oliveira 2021). It is clear a far more systemic approach is needed to realise an inclusive CE across all sectors. Governments need to address recognition and procedural injustices to enable effective participation in policy and law-making processes for communities who will be significantly impacted by structural economic reforms (see Sections 3.4.2 and 3.4.3).

The second distributive justice issue with EPR is that it could, combined with supporting contract and (intellectual) property laws, further appropriation of the global material commons by multinational corporations (Thomas 2020a; Genovese and Pansera 2021). Extracting value from material flows over their entire life cycle in an increasingly closed-loop system is the core CE objective. Yet, there is little discussion as to how, or if, the wealth generated is distributed more equitably than it is currently under the linear economy. The CE could through EPR-associated laws add to trends in the existing economy to enclose and commodify the planetary commons, including ecosystems (referred to as natural capital), aided by advances in capital-intensive technologies, especially digital (Mavropoulos and Nilsen 2020; Thompson 2020). Legal academics have already highlighted how corporations under right to repair laws are capturing value and excluding independent repair workers where digital software is installed in devices such as tractors and automated vehicles (van der Velden 2021; Perzanowski 2022). Initiatives to promote free open-source online repair manuals remain peripheral to unaffordable copyrighted manuals (Lepawsky 2020). We are yet to see how remanufacturing laws and standards will allocate rights to business, and the potential impact that these could have on access to earning opportunities for small- and medium-sized enterprises.

Distributive injustices can be minimised or avoided if effective recognition and procedural justice measures are in place. In the following two sections, we outline why recognition and procedural justice are integral for the ongoing development of CE law and policy, and the obstacles they face.

3.4.2 Recognition Justice

Increasingly pluralism is central to justice debates and how recognition injustices can be corrected. Systemic injustices are maintained by culturally specific worldviews that disregard the meanings and values of others. Narratives that inform dominant societal collective consciousness are determined by vested privileged interests within a global economic order, such as transnational corporations and the mainstream media, all that support growth-based economies. Not recognising or misrecognising other peoples and non-humans remains a core reality within the current hegemonic power structures that underpin global multilevel economic governance (Coolsaet and Neron 2021). By failing to include other worldviews, valuable knowledge and learning is not only increasingly endangered but perpetuates a disrespect towards epistemological diversity within a Western hegemonic system (Yusoff 2018; de Sousa Santos 2015). It is increasingly argued for instance that indigenous peoples' knowledge is key to how we are going to survive the ecological crisis (Norgaard and Fenlon 2021) (see Section 5.3.4).

CE discourse and initiatives are largely dominated by experts, technicians, scientists, transnational lobby organisations, governments, capital cities, and multinational enterprises, mainly in the Global North, who rely primarily on existing legal tools to advance a specific vision globally (Hobson 2016). China, who is also a major CE player, similarly privileges techno-scientific elites and government in a system of national top-down planning and developing law and policy (Luo and Leipold 2021). The revisionist nature of CE law and policy will not radically disrupt existing power relations. For example, a recent proposal for a global roadmap for an inclusive CE that would work through interconnections between existing international governance domains including trade, environment, human rights, and private legal regimes on investment and finance could potentially embed long-standing recognition and procedural inequities, especially for women and marginalised peoples (Schröder and Barrie 2022). We now consider human rights which are seen by many as a performative space within which recognition rights can be exercised. Since 1945 rights, including those for women, children, disabled, religious, and indigenous peoples have received recognition, while rights to be free from discrimination, torture, sexual violence as well as rights to freedom of expression, protest, fair trials, and many more have been adopted internationally and in numerous states incorporated into national laws. Yet, many argue that epistemological limitations, especially the colonial roots, of human rights as a framework hinder representational diversity due to normative and procedural barriers. Indeed, Samson (2020) goes so far as to argue that human rights needs to be decolonised. While de Sousa Santos and Martins (2021) claim that 'envisaging human rights as part of a collective of languages of dignity would [require] a profound understanding of the voices (the cries and murmurs), struggles (resistance and riots), memories (traumatic and triumphant), and bodies (wounded and insubmissive) of those subalternized by modern hierarchies based on capitalism, colonialism and patriarchy'.

The roots of contemporary recognition justice theory lie in Hegelian ethics, critical theory, and post and decolonial studies. Benhabib (2008) critically noted that leading theorist John Rawls, for example, in his universal work Law of People's ignored the devastation of empire and horrific realities of colonialism in framing contemporary justice claims. Fanon (1970) argued that systemic misrecognition is a symptomatic disease of the colonial relationship. While decolonial scholars argue that justice theory is mainly framed by worldviews and knowledge processes from Global North, and as such does not recognise or misrecognises other epistemologies (de Sousa Santos 2015; Escobar 2018). As such if all people are to be recognised justice needs to be decolonised. There needs to be 'cognitive justice' that recognises plural ways of understanding relationships between the world and human and non-human societies (Rodriguez 2020; Celermajer et al. 2021). If the CE is to address issues relating to justice, it needs to begin by drawing on the learning from critiques, especially from those most misrepresented and excluded under existing Western justice perspectives (Whyte 2020). Ongoing misrecognition could lead to an unjust and inequitable CE globally. A more radical approach needs to be adopted if embedded misrecognition injustices within normative institutional and legal systems are not to be carried into a CE. Moving towards greater recognition justice will require intersectional research and governance methodologies to be adopted to build spaces for understanding and communication for those who have historically suffered misrepresentation or no representation.

Achieving recognition justice will need a commitment by all those engaged in taking forward a CE. Efforts will need to be complimented by procedural justice. In the final section, we take stock of the challenges to securing procedural justice within a CE in today's international order.

3.4.3 Procedural Justice

Although several specific CE laws, such as South Korea's Framework Act on Resources Circulation, Japan's Basic Act for Establishing a Sound-Material-Cycle Society, as well as the EU Action Plan, recognise that different stakeholders are at the forefront of creating a CE, they lack specifics on the procedures on how to ensure participation is just and effective (see Section 2.2.2). This is a problem. Structural inequities in governance perpetuate exclusions from decision-making processes at all levels. So not only is there a need to focus on addressing recognition justice but also procedural justice. Effective procedural processes can provide opportunities to influence a decision-making process, outcomes, and implementation (Suiseeya 2020). As we have shown the CE is a multilevel polycentric phenomenon occurring at the micro, meso, and macro levels in both public and private spheres.

There are as such significant temporal and spatial procedural justice challenges for a global CE transformation. Decision-making in one place may have consequences for stakeholders in other jurisdictions, as well as future generations, unless an inclusive procedural approach is adopted.

In 2022 at the UN Stockholm +50, an Agenda for Change was adopted. The Agenda recognised the need for multilevel transitions to circularity across the global economy (para 6. UN Stockholm +50 2022). It was also recognised that to do so trust, cooperation, and solidarity needed to be rebuilt between states as well as non-state actors communities, youth, women, indigenous peoples, rural communities, and interfaith groups (para 7. UN Stockholm +50 2022) at a time when the multilateral systems need to be reinforced and reinvigorated (para 8. UN Stockholm +50 2022). The challenges to creating a procedurally inclusive approach for CE transitions are significant in today's geopolitical and economic climate where relations between superpowers are tense and the opportunity to exercise political rights in many countries are being curtailed by authoritarian populist regimes. However, the obstacles to advancing effective procedural justice go well-beyond current issues. The established transnational legal and governance system is increasingly criticised for a failure to adequately address long-standing procedural and recognition flaws, especially from decolonial and ecological justice scholars (de Sousa Santos 2015; Kotzé 2016).

Not all processes improve procedural justice, in part, this can be due to weak recognition justice and a persistent failure to address structural power inequities. Procedural injustices within the existing transnational governance systems although well-documented remain. Indeed, it could be argued that they are deliberately maintained to elite minority interests can be prioritised to the exclusion of the majority. Some argue that the CE is primarily being shaped and promoted by powerful stakeholders through transnational organisations, such as the Ellen MacArthur Foundation, the World Economic Forum, McKinsey, and multinational corporations (Hobson 2016; Genovese and Pansera 2021). There are also numerous transnational CE think-tanks and networks operating internationally and regionally, many of which are supported by and aligned with the leading powerful stakeholders.[1] It is argued that although many transnational processes often create participation opportunities that these do not result in influential engagement because of access, representation, and participants' capabilities limitations. As a result, participatory processes can become technocratic and apolitical procedural systems that do not lead to effective influence (Suiseeya 2020; see Section 5.4.1). As such inequities and injustices remain embedded within governance systems to the detriment of those from previously excluded communities who did participate in processes to design them.

3.4.4 Summary

Legal interventions always have impacts on social justice, and CE laws and policies will be no different. In this section, we have used Schlosberg's environmental justice tripartite approach; distribution, recognition, and procedural, as a framework to take stock of the challenges CE-related laws design and implementation face in the future. To date, distributional impacts have not been fully incorporated into research on laws being designed and implemented to advance a CE. Neither has research on law and CE focused on recognition and procedural justice dimensions. Given the exponential increase in engagement globally in the CE all three aspects of justice discourse, i.e. distributional, recognition, and procedural, need to be prioritised by both law and policy researchers, as well as advocacy organisations.

3.5 Conclusion

The CE is being established using the existing linear economy's legal infrastructure. Laws that created the linear economy have roots that go back to colonialism and the origins of today's global trade interrelationships. Embedded within global economic legal infrastructure are long-standing injustices and inequities that remain evident today. To date, there is not only limited attention within related law and policy research of the social equity aspects that need to be considered in the design and implementation of a CE transition, but neither is there an appreciation of the historical origins of current injustices. In this chapter, we have outlined the current narrow research agenda within CE law and policy scholarship. The chapter demonstrates current and historical inequities and injustices that economic laws have created over an extended period since colonialism. The final section focused on how the design of laws for a global CE needs to address long-standing distributional, recognition, and procedural injustices if it is to avoid perpetuating or even exacerbating the current disparities.

In the next two chapters, using case studies, we show in greater detail how laws and policies adopted to enable a transition to CEs appear to be failing to grasp the opportunity to address distribution, recognition, and procedural injustices in the linear economic system.

Note

1 Transnational CE thinktanks and networks operating internationally and regionally include: World Circular Economy Forum; Platform for Accelerating the Circular Economy (PACE); the African Circular Economy Network (ACEN); Latin America and the Caribbean Circular Economy Coalition (LACCEC); and the EU sponsored Global Alliance on Circular Economy and Resource Efficiency (GACERE).

References

Amorim de Oliveira, Í. 2021. Environmental justice and circular economy: analyzing justice for waste pickers in upcoming circular economy in Fortaleza, Brazil. *Circular Economy and Sustainability*, *1*(3), pp.815–834. https://doi.org/10.1007/s43615-021-00045-w.

Anghie, A. 2005. *Imperialism, Sovereignty and the Making of International Law*. Cambridge University Press.

Baars, G. 2019. *The Corporation, Law and Capitalism: A Radical Perspective on the Role of Law in the Global Political Economy*. Brill.

Barrie, J. and Schröder, P. 2021. Circular economy and international trade: a systematic literature review. *Circular Economy and Sustainability*, 2, pp.447–471. https://doi.org/10.1007/s43615-021-00126-w.

Bauwens, T., Hekkert, M. and Kirchherr, J. 2020 Circular futures: what will they look like? *Ecological Economics*, 175, p.106703. https://doi.org/10.1016/j.ecolecon.2020.106703.

Beheshti, R. 2020. The circular economy and the implied terms of contract in English sales law. *Journal of Property, Planning and Environmental Law*, 13(1), pp.31–45. https://doi.org/10.1108/JPPEL-09-2020-0042.

Benhabib, S. 2008. The legitimacy of human rights. *Daedalus*, 137(3), pp.94–104.

Blomsma, F. and Brennan, G. 2017. The emergence of circular economy: a new framing around prolonging resource productivity. *Journal of Industrial Ecology*, 21(3), pp.603–614. https://doi.org/10.1111/jiec.12603.

Carenzo, S., Juarez, P. and Becerra, L. 2022 Is there room for a circular economy "from below"? Reflections on privatisation and commoning of circular waste loops in Argentina. *Local Environment*, 1–17. https://doi.org/10.1080/13549839.2022.2048258.

Celermajer, D., Schlosberg, D., Rickards, L., Stewart-Harawira, M., Thaler, M., Tschakert, P., Verlie, C. and Winter, C. 2021. Multispecies justice: theories, challenges, and a research agenda for environmental politics. *Environmental Politics*, 30(1, 2), 119–140. https://doi.org/10.1080/09644016.2020.1827608.

Chateau, J., and Mavroeidi, E. 2020. *The Jobs Potential of a Transition Towards a Resource Efficient and Circular Economy*. OECD Environment Working Papers.

Chibber, V. 2014. *Postcolonial Theory and the Specter of Capital*. Verso Books.

Chimni, B.S. 2013. Critical theory and international economic law: a third world approach to international law (TWAIL) perspective. *Research Handbook on Global Justice and International Economic Law*, pp.251–273. Edward Elgar Publishing.

Circle Economy. 2022. *Circularity Gap Report 2022*. Amsterdam: Platform for Accelerating the Circular Economy. https://www.circularity-gap.world/.

Coolsaet, B. and Neron, P. 2021. Recognition and environmental justice. In: Coolsaet, B. (Ed.), *Environmental Justice: Key Issues*. Routledge.

Cullet, P. 2016. Differential treatment in environmental law: addressing critiques and conceptualizing the next steps. *Transnational Environmental Law*, 5(2), pp.305–328.

de Sousa Santos, B. 2002. *Toward a New Legal Common Sense: Law, Globalization, and Emancipation*. Cambridge University Press

de Sousa Santos, B. 2015. *Epistemologies of the South: Justice against Epistemicide*. Routledge.

de Sousa Santos, B. and Martins, B.S. 2021. *The Pluriverse of Human Rights: The Diversity of Struggles for Dignity*. Routledge.

Ekins, P., Domenech, T., Drummond, P., Bleischwitz, R., Hughes, N. and Lotti, L. 2019 *The Circular Economy: What, Why, How and Where?* Background paper for an OECD/EC Workshop. www.oecd.org/cfe/regionaldevelopment/Ekins-2019-Circular-Economy-What-Why-How-Where.pdf.

Elhacham, E., Ben-Uri, L., Grozovski, J., Bar-On, Y.M. and Milo, R. 2020. Global human-made mass exceeds all living biomass. *Nature*, 588, pp.442–444. https://doi.org/10.1038/s41586-020-3010-5.

Escobar, A. 2018. Transition discourses and the politics of relationality: towards designs for the pluriverse. In Reiter, B. (Ed.), *Constructing the Pluriverse: The Geopolitics of Knowledge*, pp.63–89. Duke University Press.

Eslava, L. 2015. *Local Space, Global Life*. Cambridge University Press.

Fanon, F. 1970. *Black Skin, White Masks*. Paladin.

Frerichs, S. 2013. Law, economy and society in the global age: a study guide. In: Perry-Kessaris (Ed.), *Socio-Legal Approaches to International Economic Law*, pp.50–64. Routledge.

Friant, M.C., Vermeulen, W.J. and Salomone, R. 2020. A typology of circular economy discourses: navigating the diverse visions of a contested paradigm. *Resources, Conservation and Recycling*, 161, p.104917. https://doi.org/10.1016/j.resconrec.2020.104917.

Geng, Y., Sarkis, J. and Bleischwitz, R. 2019. How to globalize the circular economy. *Nature*, 565, pp.153–155. https://doi.org/10.1038/d41586-019-00017-z.

Genovese, A. and Pansera, M. 2021. The circular economy at a crossroad: technocratic eco-modernism or convivial technology for social revolution? *Capitalism Nature Socialism*, 32(2), pp.95–113. https://doi.org/10.1080/10455752.2020.1763414.

Ghosh, A. 2021. *The Nutmeg's Curse: Parables for a Planet in Crisis*. University of Chicago Press.

Gonzalez, C.G. 2001. Beyond eco-imperialism: an environmental justice critique of free trade. *Denver University Law Review*, 78, pp.979–1016.

Gonzalez, C.G. 2015. Bridging the North-South divide: international environmental law in the Anthropocene. *Pace Environmental Law Review*, 32(2), pp.407–433.

Hardoon, D. and Slater, J. 2015. *Inequality and the End of Extreme Poverty*. Oxfam. https://policy-practice.oxfam.org/resources/inequality-and-the-end-of-extreme-poverty-577506/.

Hobson, K. 2016. Closing the loop or squaring the circle? Locating generative spaces for the circular economy. *Progress in Human Geography*, 40(1), pp.88–104. https://doi.org/10.1177/0309132514566342.

ILO (International Labour Organisation). 2018. *Women and Men in the Informal Economy: A Statistical Picture*, 3rd ed. https://www.ilo.org/global/publications/books/WCMS_626831/lang--en/index.htm.

Kaswan, A. 2021. Distributive environmental justice. In: Coolsaet, B. (Ed.). *Environmental Justice: Key issues*. Routledge.

Kojola, E. and Pellow, D.N. 2021. New directions in environmental justice studies: examining the state and violence. *Environmental Politics*, 30(1, 2), pp.100–118.

Kotzé, L.J. 2016. *Global Environmental Constitutionalism in the Anthropocene*. Bloomsbury Publishing.

Lepawsky, J. 2020. Planet of fixers? Mapping the middle grounds of independent and do-it-yourself information and communication technology maintenance and repair. *Geo: Geography and Environment*, 7(1), p.e00086. https://doi.org/10.1002/geo2.86.

Luo, A. and Leipold, S. 2021. Chinese lessons on upscaling environmental policy concepts: a review of policy-oriented circular economy research. *Journal of Cleaner Production*, 333, p.130047. https://doi.org/10.1016/j.jclepro.2021.130047.

Martuzzi, M., Mitis, F. and Forastiere, F. 2010. Inequalities, inequities, environmental justice in waste management and health. *European Journal of Public Health*, 20(1), pp.21–26.

Mattei, U. and Nader, L. 2008. *Plunder: When the Rule of Law is Illegal*. John Wiley & Sons.

Mavropoulos, A., and Nilsen, A.W. 2020. *Industry 4.0 and Circular Economy: Towards a Wasteless Future or a Wasteful Planet?* Wiley.

Mickelson, K. 2005. Leading towards a level playing field, repaying ecological debt, or making environmental space: three stories about international environmental cooperation. *Osgoode Hall Law Journal*, 43, pp.137–170.

Miles, K. 2010 International investment law: origins, imperialism and conceptualizing the environment. *Colorado Journal of International Environmental Law and Policy*, 21(1), pp.21, 22.

Natarajan, U. and Khoday, K. 2014. *Locating Nature: Making and Unmaking International Law*. Cambridge University Press.

Nixon, R. 2011. *Slow Violence and the Environmentalism of the Poor*. Harvard University Press.

Norgaard, K.M. and Fenelon, J.V. 2021. Towards an indigenous environmental sociology. In: Caniglia, B.S., Jorgenson, A., Malin, S.A., Peel, L., Pellow, D.N. and Huang, X. (Eds.), *Handbook of Environmental Sociology*, pp. 477–494. Springer.

Oberle, B., Bringezu, S., Hatfield-Dodds, S., Hellweg, S., Schandl, H., Clement, J., et al. 2019. *Global Resources Outlook 2019: Natural Resources for the Future We Want*. https://wedocs.unep.org/handle/20.500.11822/27517.

OECD. 2016. *Extended Producer Responsibility: Guidance for Efficient Waste Management*. www.oecd.org/environment/waste/Extended-producer-responsibility-Policy-Highlights2016-web.pdf.

PACE (Partnership for Action on Green Economy). 2017. Green Jobs Assessment Institutions Network (GAIN) 3rd International Conference: Just Transition. Report and Conclusions. www.un-page.org/resources/green-jobs/green-jobs-assessments-just-transition.

Paredis, E. 2009. *The Concept of Ecological Debt: Its Meaning and Applicability in International Policy*. Academia Press.

Patnaik, U. and Patnaik, P. 2021. *Capital and Imperialism: Theory, History, and the Present*. Monthly Review Press.

Pekkarinen, V., Toussaint, P. and van Asselt, H. 2019. Loss and damage after Paris: Moving beyond rhetoric. *Carbon and Climate Law Review*, 13(1), pp.31–49.

Perrone, N.M. and Schneiderman, D. 2019. International economic law's wreckage: depoliticization, inequality, precarity. In: *Research Handbook on Critical Legal Theory*. Edward Elgar Publishing.

Perzanowski, A. 2022. *The Right to Repair: Reclaiming the Things we Own*. Cambridge University Press.

Piketty, T. 2015. *The Economics of Inequality*. Harvard: Harvard University Press.

Pistor, K. 2019. *The Code of Capital*. Princeton University Press.

Preston, F., Lehne, J. and Wellesley, L. 2019. *An Inclusive Circular Economy: Priorities for Developing Countries*. The Royal Institute of International Affairs. www.chathamhouse.org/2019/05/inclusive-circular-economy.

Rajamani, L. 2006. *Differential Treatment in International Environmental Law*. Oxford University Press.

Reams, M.A. and Templet, P.H. 1996. Political and environmental equity issues related to municipal waste incineration siting. *Journal of Hazardous Materials*, 47, pp.313–323.

Reike, D, Vermeulen, J.V. and Witjes, S. 2018. The circular economy: new or refurbished as CE 3.0?—exploring controversies in the conceptualization of the circular economy through a focus on history and resource value retention options. *Resources, Conservation and Recycling*, 135, pp.246–264. https://doi.org/10.1016/j.resconrec.2017.08.027.

Repp, L. Hekkert, M. and Kirchherr, J. 2021. Circular economy-induced global employment shifts in apparel value chains: job reduction in apparel production activities, job growth in reuse and recycling activities. *Resources,*

Conservation and Recycling, 171, pp.13–18. https://doi.org/10.1016/j. resconrec.2021.105621.

Robinson, S.A. and Carlson, D.A. 2021. A just alternative to litigation: applying restorative justice to climate-related loss and damage. *Third World Quarterly*, 42(6), pp.1384–1395. https://doi.org/10.1080/01436597.2021. 1877128.

Rodriguez, I. 2020. The Latin American decolonial environmental justice approach. In: Brendan, C. (Ed.), *Environmental Justice. Key Issues.* Earthscan from Routledge.

Samson, C. 2020. *The Colonialism of Human Rights: Ongoing Hypocrisies of Western Liberalism.* John Wiley & Sons.

Scherer, L., Behrens, P., de Koning, A., Heijungs, R., Sprecher, B. and Tukker, A. 2018. Trade-offs between social and environmental Sustainable Development Goals. *Environmental Science and Policy*, 90, pp.65–72.

Schlosberg, D. 2004. Reconceiving environmental justice: global movements and political theories. *Environmental Politics*, 13(3), pp.517–540. https://doi. org/10.1080/0964401042000229025.

Schröder, P. and Barrie, J.A. 2022. *Global Roadmap for an Inclusive Circular Economy.* www.renewablematter.eu/articles/article/a-global-roadmap-for-an-inclusive-circular-economy.

Schröder, P., Lemille, A. and Desmond, P. 2020. Making the circular economy work for human development. *Resources, Conservation and Recycling*, 156, p.104686. https://doi.org/10.1016/j.resconrec.2020.104686.

Suiseeya, K.R.M. 2020. Procedural justice matters: Power, representation, and participation in environmental governance. In: Coolsaet, B. (Ed.), *Environmental Justice*, pp.37–51. Routledge.

Talbott, T.C. 2022. Extended Producer Responsibility: opportunities and challenges for waste pickers. In: Alfers, L., Chen, M. and Plagerson, S. (Eds.), *Social Contracts and Informal Workers in the Global South*, pp.126–143. Cheltenham: Edward Elgar. https://doi.org/10.4337/9781839108068.00013.

Thomas, F.A. 2019a. *The Global Informal Economy: Large but on the Decline.* IMF. https://blogs.imf.org/2019/10/30/the-global-informal-economy-large-but-on-the-decline/.

Thomas, S. 2019b. Law and the circular economy. *Journal of Business Law*, 1, pp.62–83.

Thomas, S. 2020a. Waste, marginal property practices and the circular economy. *Journal of Property, Planning and Environmental Law*, 12(3), pp.203–218. https://doi.org/10.1108/JPPEL-02-2020-0012.

Thomas, S. 2020b. Legal considerations for a circular economy. In: Tudor, T, and Dutra, C. (Eds.), *The Routledge Handbook of Waste, Resources and the Circular Economy.* Routledge.

Thompson, R.J. 2020. *Proleptic Leadership on the Commons: Ushering in a New Global Order.* Emerald Publishing Limited. https://doi. org/10.1108/978-1-83867-799-220201005.

UN Human Rights Council. 2022. The right to a clean, healthy and sustainable environment: non-toxic environment. *Report of the Special Rapporteur on the Issue of Human Rights Obligations relating to the Enjoyment of a Safe, Clean, Healthy and Sustainable Environment.* 12 January 2022. UNDOC/ GEN/G22/004/48/PDF/G2200448.

United Nations June 2022 UN Stockholm+50 Agenda for Action, Renewal and Trust. www.stockholm50.global/resources/stockholm50-agenda-action-renewal-and-trust-outputs-and-outcomes.

UNIDO (United Nations Industrial Development Organization). 2017. *Circular Economy.* www.unido.org/sites/default/files/2017-07/Circular_Economy_UNIDO_0.pdf.

van der Velden, M. 2021. 'Fixing the world one thing at a time': community repair and a sustainable circular economy. *Journal of Cleaner Production,* 304, p.127151. https://doi.org/10.1016/j.jclepro.2021.127151.

Warlenius, R. 2016. Linking ecological debt and ecologically unequal exchange: stocks, flows, and unequal sink appropriation. *Journal of Political Ecology,* 23(1), pp.364–380. https://doi.org/10.2458/v23i1.20223.

Webster, K. 2017. *The Circular Economy: A Wealth of Flows.* Ellen MacArthur Foundation Publishing.

Whyte, K. 2018. Settler colonialism, ecology, and environmental injustice. *Environment and Society,* 9(1), pp.125–144. https://doi.org/10.3167/ares.2018.090109.

Whyte, K. 2020. Indigenous environmental justice: anti-colonial action through kinship. In: Coolsaet, B. (Ed.), *Environmental Justice.* Routledge.

Williams. M., Schroeder, P., Gower, R., Kendal, J., Retamal, M., Dominish, E. and Green, J. 2018. *Bending the Curve: Best Practice Interventions for the Circular Economy in Developing Countries.* Tearfund. https://learn.tearfund.org/-/media/learn/resources/reports/2018-tearfund-bending-the-curve-en.pdf.

Woggsborg, A. and Schröder, P. 2018. Nigeria's e-waste management: extended producer responsibility and informal sector inclusion. *Journal of Waste Resources and Recycling,* 1(1), pp.1–9. https://doi.org/10.15744/2766-5887.1.102.

Yamaguchi, S. 2018. *International trade and the transition to a more resource efficient and circular economy a concept paper.* OECD Trade and Environment Working Papers 2018/03. https://doi.org/10.1787/847feb24-en.

Yusoff, K. 2018. A *Billion Black Anthropocenes or None.* University of Minnesota Press.

Zink, T. and Geyer, R. 2017. Circular economy rebound. *Journal of Industrial Ecology,* 21(3), pp.593–602. https://doi.org/10.1111/jiec.12545.

4   Circular Plastics Economy

The majority of plastic waste reuse, recycling, and recovery operations continues to cause significant environmental harm from air pollution to water contamination. The core challenge for those trying to create a circular plastics sector is to avoid adopting solution-based responses rooted in 'same-but-circular-business' models. To incentivise a circular plastics economy regulatory measures are needed to. In this chapter, we examine examples of both bottom-up and top-down regulatory approaches used to achieve circular plastics economies.

4.1 Introduction

Despite mass production of plastics only beginning around six decades ago, more than eight billion metric tonnes of plastics have been created since, with most ending up as 'wasted' waste (Parker 2018). This is only expected to increase. Ocean Conservancy and McKinsey Center for Business and Environment (2015) project that oceans may contain one tonne of plastic for every three tonnes of finfish by 2025. Similarly, The Pew Charitable Trusts and SYSTEMIQ (2020) estimate the annual flow of plastic into the ocean will nearly triple by 2040 unless mitigating steps are taken. The majority (79%) of plastic wastes produced accumulates in landfills or leaks (i.e., unmanaged release) into the natural environment (predominantly oceans) (Geyer et al. 2017; Parker 2018). Landfills can cause soil, groundwater, surface water, and air pollution, because of methane gas released by wastes accompanied by other pollutants containing characteristic toxins of deposited waste, which impact human health (Westlake 1995; Mulholland and Dyer 1999). Leakage similarly harms human health with, for example, initial evidence of plastics entering the human food chain (Waluda and Staniland 2013; Allouzi et al. 2021).[1]

DOI: 10.4324/9780429355141-4

One of the myriad issues with plastics and their wastes is that the life expectancy of many plastics is less than one year (Payne and Jones 2021). Additionally, many of the commonly used plastics are not biodegradable and result in 'near-permanent contamination of the natural environment' (Geyer et al. 2017) – some types of plastics take more than 400 years to degrade (Rochman et al. 2016; Parker 2018). Plastics are therefore an intergenerational issue, as plastics produced and disposed of today will continue to impact not only current but also future generations.

There is no global agreed definition of plastic wastes, even though plastics are covered in provisions of some international and supranational agreements on waste. These include the Basel Convention on the Control of Transboundary Movements of Hazardous Wastes and Their Disposal (Basel Convention), Convention on the Prevention of Marine Pollution by Dumping of Wastes and Other Matter (London Convention), EU Waste Framework Directive (2008/98/EC), and Bamako Convention on the Ban of the Import into Africa and the Control of Transboundary Movement and Management of Hazardous Wastes within Africa. The London Convention, for example, prohibits the dumping of persistent plastics in the marine environment, but does not define it (Art. IV.1). The lack of definition may be due to the existence of many different types of plastics that are defined through chemical formulae (e.g., single-polymer plastics, such as polyethylene terephthalate (PET) or polypropene, and composite plastics comprising different polymer types or other materials than waste). Many types of plastic are recognised but not defined in the Basel Convention (see Annex II and IX). The lack of a definition of plastic waste has generally not been highlighted as an issue within academic literature. Likely this is because there are legal definitions of waste (see Section 1.3.1) and chemical formulae and/or set characteristics for different types of plastic. When implementing regulatory measures, the different plastic types and distinctive lifespan attributes need to be understood for appropriate treatment and management to be supported (Clift et al. 2019).

A critical tension arises from opposing perceptions of plastics as either resource or pollutant. In the following section, Section 4.2, we take a closer look at the significance of this dual conceptualisation of plastics. Even though there are beneficial uses of plastics and certain plastic wastes can (at least in part) be reused, recycled, and recovered, the focus for the purposes of achieving circular economies (CEs) should nonetheless remain on the prevention and minimisation of plastics use in their entirety. An understanding of these rivalling views of plastics therefore provides a gateway for understanding wherefrom the complexity of the governance of plastics within CEs arises. In Section 4.3, we first examine examples of bottom-up waste management (informal recycling sector and industrial symbiosis) to illustrate some of these complexities in practice, before covering international and national top-down governance of plastic wastes in Section 4.4.

4.2 Plastic Wastes: Resource or Pollutant?

There is tension between the conceptualisation of plastic wastes as pollutants that should be prevented and as 'wasted' resources that should instead be reused, recycled, or recovered. There is no consensus on what pollution comprises, though various definitions exist in different environmental texts (Van Heijnsbergen 1979). Generally, pollution is used either in relation to a specific context or to indicate an alteration to an existing environment through damage or interference (Springer 1977; Van Heijnsbergen 1979). From a legal perspective, plastic wastes can be viewed as either. Plastic waste can, for example, be a land-based source polluting the marine environment, which should be prevented, reduced, and controlled by States through laws and regulations pursuant to Art. 213 of the United Nations Convention on the Law of the Seas (UNCLOS). Current waste management operations can also result in alterations to the environment, such as plastic leakage into the natural environment or land use as landfill for plastic (and other) wastes (e.g., Lau et al. 2020). Despite this, many commentators acknowledge that the complete elimination of plastics from the modern economy is impossible and even undesirable as they have numerous beneficial uses. Plastics, for instance, extend the shelf-life of food products and thereby avoid some food waste (e.g., White and Lockyer 2020). They also benefit public health in diverse applications such as sterile packaging for medical instruments, disposable syringes, and tissue engineering (e.g., North and Halden 2013).

Some argue therefore that instead of preventing plastic wastes the focus should be on reducing plastic leakage into the environment (see Clift et al. 2019). Plastic wastes in this perspective are plastic substances that can be reused, recycled, or recovered in line with the CE concept. To capture how perceptions of plastic wastes as resources can present challenges to law and policy-making, we consider these within the distinct treatment contexts of reuse, recycling, recovery, and bioplastics.

4.2.1 Reuse

Some reuse waste management approaches have been entrenched in civil society for centuries. Research on indigenous waste management knowledge and practices includes the use of waste cans and tins to produce local items such as lanterns, funnels, and bread pans (Kosoe et al. 2019); the use of plastic containers as petrol containers by the Nenets on Kolguev Island in the high Russian Arctic (Siragusa and Arzyutov 2020); plastic bottles as vases by Veps, an indigenous group traditionally living in rural areas in Northwest Russia (Siragusa and Arzyutov 2020); and plastic waste in artwork in Nigeria (Wagner-Lawlor 2018). These examples form part of a wider informal recycling sector (see Section 4.3.1). 'Informal recycling sector' is a term used to describe individuals or other entities extracting recyclable materials from mixed municipal solid waste (Ezeah et al. 2013). Even though the term 'recycling' is used, the sector also covers reuse operations such as cleaning or repairing (see Section 1.3.2).

Some of these community reuse traditions are becoming increasingly difficult to implement as a result of modern lifestyles and adoption of modern technologies by municipal authorities and policymakers (Kosoe et al. 2019). Critically, reuse practices by the informal sector are being challenged by the private sector by importing similar, cheaper products such as plastics.

4.2.2 Recycling

More plastics are being recycled than before, but the rate of recycling is not increasing at the same rate as the amount of virgin plastics being produced (Merrington 2017). The dominant current recycling approach is mechanical recycling, which comprises washing, shredding, melting, and remoulding of plastic polymers. There are limits to mechanical recycling as plastics, unlike materials such as copper, cannot be recycled indefinitely without loss of quality. The polymers are not degraded by the process, but it is, for example, the inclusion of additives and contamination that degrades the plastic product quality (e.g., Garcia and Robertson 2017; UNPRI 2019; Kunzig 2020). Other challenges include avoiding contamination in collection and sorting of plastic wastes, and social concerns as residents near plastic recycling workshops have been found to suffer from cancer risks (He et al. 2015; Parker 2020).

Some mechanical recycling issues can be alleviated by chemical recycling (Parker 2020). Chemical recycling consists of breaking down plastic polymers into their original monomers and then rearranging these monomers to produce new material. Chemical recycling is still in its infancy and requires further development to improve its efficiency (Rahimi and García 2017; UNPRI 2019). The affordability of the process, in part due to high energy costs, is currently a critical barrier to chemical recycling becoming a widespread recycling practice. Research on increasing the efficiency and reducing the costs of the process are therefore priority areas of the research agenda on recycling (Garcia and Robertson 2017; Rahimi and García 2017).

Similar to reuse (see Section 4.2.1), there are examples of longstanding recycling practices. Kosoe et al.'s (2019) research on traditional waste management approaches in the Jaman South Municipality in Ghana highlighted the melting old (scrap) metals to create new desired items (e.g., knife, cutlass, hoe, axe, spoon) and converting used tyres into slippers and ropers for drawing water from wells. Yet, an underlying issue of both mechanical and chemical recycling hindering uptake is that plastics remain very cheap to make, while recycled and reclaimed plastic has little value. It therefore more often than not makes more business-sense to make new plastics instead of recycling plastics (Parker 2020).

4.2.3 Other Recovery

Waste-to-energy is one of the ways in which wastes, including plastics, can be recovered to reduce volume and weight of materials by destroying contaminated materials and producing energy. Recent research has focused on turning plastic wastes into hydrogen and carbon (e.g., Jie et al. 2020; Midili et al. 2021). Plastic to hydrogen processes result in less oxidant demand, flexibility of products, and high hydrogen production efficiency. They also, however, have a higher amount of tar production, higher operational cost, higher amount of carbon dioxide yield, low gasification efficiency, some impurities and pollutants, and high ash production compared to traditional combustion processes (Midili et al. 2021). In addition, more widespread general waste-to-energy operations face techno-economic (the costly development of new technologies and investment in new machinery), political/regulatory (stakeholders need a stable framework to evolve and invest in CEs), and operational (the changing quantities and properties of municipal solid waste to be energy recovered) challenges (Lausselet et al. 2017). Yet, investment continues in waste-to-energy systems.

The Korea District Heating Corporation based in South Korea, for example, has announced that it will launch a CE project to turn plastic wastes into hydrogen district heating (Byung-wook 2021). Hyundai Engineering Co., a construction unit of South Korea's Hyundai Motor Group, is also investing in plants to produce hydrogen from plastic wastes (Eun 2021). Such systems may result in lock-ins to systems based on continued generation of plastic wastes. Implementations of (plastic) waste-to-energy systems can therefore slow the emergence of more sustainable, circular infrastructures (Upham and Jones 2012; Corvellec et al. 2013).

Already discarded plastic waste can also become a resource. Landfills are being recognised as sources of man-made resources from the past waiting to be picked up and used (Burlakovs et al. 2017). The Gò Cát landfill in Ho Chi Minh City, Vietnam, for example, is discussing the potential use of existing landfill sites to generate financial resources through the valorisation of: landfill gas; materials from landfill body after landfill mining; energy produced from Gò Cát landfill body after landfill mining; land recycling after deconstruction of Gò Cát landfill; and landfill surface through a biomass utilisation plant in case the landfill remains (Schneider et al. 2017). There are also initiatives to use leaked plastic wastes as resources. The Plastic Bank, for instance, is an initiative that rewards people without access to banks with a bespoke type of cryptocurrency-based token for bringing ocean-bound plastic waste to recycling centres. The Plastic Bank currently operates in Brazil, Egypt, Indonesia, and the Philippines, with franchise-based expansion in Cameroon and Thailand. The collected plastics are reprocessed into feedstock, which is then reused by companies in manufacturing products and packaging.[2]

Plastic wastes recovery using waste-to-energy or recovery of landfilled and leaked plastic wastes are problematic because such processes are typically operationalised in a way that promotes commodification of plastic wastes by assigning value to them (see Section 1.3.2). If incinerating waste and recovery of landfilled and leaked plastic wastes can result in financial gains, there may be no incentives to reduce consumption of plastics and generation of plastic wastes. This is not to suggest that all cases of recovering landfilled or leaked plastic waste are financially motivated. In Rotterdam in the Netherlands, for instance, littered plastic bottles are removed from the Nieuwe Maas, a distributary of the Rhine, and used to build a floating island for communal use without an underlying financial value creation model.[3]

4.2.4 Redesigning Plastics: Bioplastics

At the start-of-life of many plastics, fossil fuels are used as raw feedstocks. Even though there are an increasing number of innovations that produce plastics from organic materials (e.g., Ecovatic makes packaging from organic materials; a Chilean start-up, Algramo, is working to replace single-serve packets), there is currently insufficient research on their life cycle assessment and environmental impacts (Narancic and O'Connor 2019; White and Lockyer 2020).

Bioplastics (also known as biopolymers) are plastics that are both biobased and biodegradable. Mandating the use of bioplastics may prevent issues of permanence caused by other plastic wastes leaking into the natural environment. The time in which the polymers biodegrade is, however, highly affected by the environments in which they biodegrade (e.g., many will not biograde in landfill) and the bioplastics' physical and chemical structures (Emadian et al. 2017; Parker 2020). Research also highlights that bioplastics are not necessarily more environmentally sound than other plastics. Tabone et al. (2010), for example, examined 12 different polymers (derived from petroleum, petroleum sources, and biological sources) and biopolymers. Biopolymers neither ranked highest based on environmental impacts nor did they consistently perform best in relation to environmental metrics. Bioplastics resulted in the greatest amounts of pollutants in their study (likely because of fertilisers and pesticides used in their production), though performed better in terms of lower greenhouse gas emissions (Tabone et al. 2010).

4.2.5 Summary

Plastic wastes can be conceived as a pollutant or resource. Plastics have many beneficial uses, but resultant wastes and their management cause pollution (e.g., landfill, incineration, and leakage into the natural environment). Many options that frame plastic wastes as resources through reuse, recycling, and recovery exist or are being developed, but even these can result in pollution. Bioplastics have been touted as an alternative to address current issues of plastic wastes, yet further research is needed to understand their impacts compared to traditional plastics. Moreover, the focus on reuse, recycling, recovery, and bioplastics is solution-based, whereas we need to focus on the problem of waste prevention through tackling production processes and (over-)consumption. This presents a very tough challenge crystallised by the structures of the linear economic system (Parker

2020; see Chapter 3). Current and proposed bottom-up and top-down governance approaches have sought to address some of these challenges and are examined in the following sections.

4.3 Bottom-Up Circular Plastics Governance

Bottom-up approaches to resource governance can support waste management strategies by incorporating local characteristics, customs, waste composition, and other evidence (Agamuthu et al. 2009). Many initiatives have evolved over time, though the coronavirus (SARS-CoV2) pandemic demonstrated the flexibility and elasticity of bottom-up approaches for rapidly implementing initiatives embodying CE principles. For instance, during early coronavirus outbreaks, breweries produced disinfection alcohol from residue products and individual citizens made mouth masks from textile leftovers to address shortages and reduce import dependency (Wuyts et al. 2020).

In this section, we use two case studies of circular use of plastic wastes – informal recycling sector and industrial symbiosis – to provide additional examples of bottom-up governance initiatives and elucidate related justice issues with these.

4.3.1 Informal Recycling Sector

The informal recycling sector has been described as symbiotic with CEs, because waste pickers (also described as waste scavengers) view waste as a resource (Ezeah et al. 2013). Evidence even suggests that waste pickers recycle more than the entire formal waste management industry combined (Cook and Velis 2020; Velis 2021). Academic scholarship provides a range of more detailed accounts of the experiences and activities of these waste pickers. Ogwueleke and BP (2021), for instance, report on price exploitation and social stigmatisation challenges faced by waste pickers in North-Central Nigeria, who recover high-value plastics (e.g., PET, polystyrene) to sell, whereas Yang et al. (2018) examined the health hazards faced by waste pickers in well-established informal plastics (especially bottles) recycling sectors in Delhi and Beijing. See preceding sections for additional examples of informal recycling sector activities.

The high volume of plastic wastes produced raises critical environmental, health, and safety issues for informal recycling workers. Environmental hazards arise from the open-air burning of plastic wastes, which releases dangerous chemicals and particulates (soot and solid ash residue) (Oyegunle and Thompson 2018). Health hazards include mechanical (e.g., traumas, fractures, lacerations), ergonometric (e.g., musculoskeletal illness), chemical (e.g., dermatitis, respiratory diseases), biological (e.g., diarrhoea, intestinal worms, leptospirosis), and social (e.g., malnourishment, under-nourishment) impacts (Gutberlet and Baeder 2008; Penteado and de Castro 2021). Safety and well-being issues extend to unprotected children in dumpsites, perpetuated by unsafe working conditions and social stigma associated with manually handling waste (Velis 2021).

Environmental, health, and safety hazards and risks are part of the reasons for why it is typical that informal waste recycling is carried out by poor, disadvantaged, vulnerable, and/or marginalised social groups (e.g., gypsies, rural migrants, disabled, elderly, the illiterate, and religious minorities) who resort to scavenging for income generation (Ezeah et al. 2013). There are different categories of informal recyclers reflecting different roles and characteristics. These range from household waste collectors to street pickers to dumpsite pickers to middlemen (Ojeda-Benitez et al. 2002; Ezeah et al. 2013). Bening et al.'s (2022) study on informal plastic waste management in Accra, Ghana, combines multiple sources of evidence that show street waste pickers as the poorest and most vulnerable, earning only a fraction of the already low minimum wage, whereas middlemen and aggregators receive higher earnings, for which they are criticised, but also provide social-security-like services to waste pickers. Other investigations into distributional equity issues within the informal sector in the informal plastic further reveal plastic waste cases where the welfare of public and employees is disregarded (Goldstein 2016).

The most glaring justice issues result from the formal/informal recycling sector division itself. The existence of the formal/informal sector division translates into unequal access to the benefits of the waste-generating activities, and unequal vulnerability to hazards and exploitation risks to persons and communities at either side of that divide. Using a detailed case study of Wenan's informal recycling sector plastics in China, Goldstein (2016) argues that 'the formal/informal division is a persistently reinforced and malleable policy tool, regularly reinvented and renewed to show up privileged political, administrative, and business networks against a wide range of outsiders (who are often, not coincidentally, business competitors) by labelling them not just as vaguely inferior (uncivilised, un-modern), but as polluting criminals. So branded, informal enterprises can be shut down at any moment, their assets confiscated and destroyed without compensation, conditions that predictably result in informal shops cutting costs in ways that negatively impact the environment and health'. He cautions that policies criminalising the informal waste and recycling sector to eliminate these issues result in a 'race to the bottom' instead of preventing it. Similarly, governance responses that focus on prevention of plastic wastes ignore that individual citizens may rely on continued plastic waste for their income.

There has been success in establishing alternative governance approaches that avoid some of these misplaced regulatory interventions and better accommodate the needs and rights or informal waste pickers. In Brazil, India, Mexico, Colombia, and New York City, informal recyclers have formed cooperatives, gaining municipal and at times national recognition, and become legitimised channels for collecting and processing recyclers (Goldstein 2016). Rather than approaching informal businesses and workers as law-breaking antagonists to desirable development, they are reperceived as potential collaborators whose skills, resources, and interests can be engaged to help solve environmental and health problems – problems that affect them directly (Gunsilius et al. 2011; Goldstein 2016; see also Wilson et al. 2006).

4.3.2 *Industrial Symbiosis*

The private sector has played a significant role in the development of alternative bottom-up waste management approaches. Many private sector consumer good companies, including Nestle, Unilever, Coca-Cola, and Danone, have made individual commitments engaging with plastic waste issues. There has also been coordinated action between private sector actors, such as a group of leading companies, such as Honeywell, Shell, and Veolia, forming the Alliance to End Plastic Waste, committing USD 1.5 billion over next five years (Alliance to End Plastic Waste 2019).

The formation of bottom-up approaches is not always coordinated from the outset by the actors involved, however, and often they emerge over time periods that span years and decades. An emblematic illustration of such organically evolving bottom-up waste management approaches is encountered in many practical realisations of industrial symbiosis. Industrial symbiosis is a description of arrangements in which organisations exchange wastes (and by-products) to generate economic, environmental, and social benefits (Chertow 2007). There are several examples of industrial symbiosis networks being promoted through use of the law both at national and local levels across the Global North and South. Prominent examples in which legal instruments made significant contribution to industrial symbiosis initiation are found in the Global North Australia and Denmark, and in the Global South China, India, South Korea, and Mexico.

Arguably the most widely studied example of plastic wastes use within industrial symbiosis networks is found in Kawasaki in Japan. Here, plastic wastes are recycled into a reductant for blast furnace processes, as well as collected from a home appliance recycling facility and urban area to be used as deoxidisation matter for making steel products and cement production (Hashimoto et al. 2010; Dong et al. 2013). The translation of an industrial symbiosis configuration from one context to another to recreate its bottom-up governance effects is, however, limited in practice. Dong et al. (2013) examined how some of lessons from Kawasaki could be used in China, but found problems with plastics flows: different contents and fluctuating quantity of plastic wastes meant the resultant operational uncertainties made replication of the Kawasaki bottom-up governance unviable. The combined issue presented by the low cost of plastics from primary raw materials and reduced quality of recycled plastics presents another barrier to industrial symbiosis development initiatives (Krivtsov et al. 2004). Similar localisation challenges and lessons have been reported on the Global South, as with the Flying Tree Environmental Management plastics industrial symbiosis cluster in Trinidad and Tobago (Mahabir et al. 2020).

4.3.3 Summary

Bottom-up approaches to waste management come in many forms and styles. Some configurations and arrangements are actively coordinated between private and/or public actors, while others emerge more haphazardly. The examples shared of diverse experiences with bottom-up approaches in both informal waste picking as well as industrial symbiosis contexts highlight that various equity issues persist across all these forms and styles, irrespective of their development patterns. Explorations of other innovations in bottom-up approaches would no doubt further put into focus additional equity issues. Some of the recent trends in bottom-up waste governance using technological advances such as for example blockchain technology seek to explicitly address inequities in access to financial capital to participate in the plastics CE (e.g., Plastic Bank 2022; see Steenmans et al. 2021). A constant across all these approaches is the critical role of the pricing of waste in driving behaviour change.

4.4 Top-Down Circular Plastics Governance

In parallel to bottom-up approaches, a wide range of top-down circular plastics governance practices have been developed and implemented over recent years. Such top-down approaches typically see a more central role of public actors and institutions, developing, coordinating, and enforcing activities across international, national, and local levels of governance.

4.4.1 International Level

The term 'waste colonialism' was coined in the late 1980s and early 1990s to describe the practices by high gross domestic product (GDP) countries of dumping toxic wastes in low GDP countries with few technological or regulatory means to deal with that waste (Sridhar and Kumar 2019).[4] High GDP countries fail to recognise the power imbalance imposed within this practice through arguing that low GDP countries can ban waste imports. It is further argued that the export of wastes provided low GDP countries with economic benefits, such as employment generation and cheap material recovery (Sridhar and Kumar 2019). Yet, the nature of transboundary movements of wastes as a form of colonialism is further underlined by the indirect access to land that it enables, where high GDP countries essentially shift their landfill to low GDP countries (Akpan and Inyang 2017; Liboiron 2018; Sridhar and Kumar 2019). Waste colonialism, including plastic waste colonialism, continues to be a large-scale stressor in international plastic wastes management, as recently demonstrated by the disruptive impacts China's 2017 Operation National Sword ban on the import of certain plastic wastes had on the waste streams of high GDP countries.

International negotiations around waste colonialism partially motivated adoption of the Basel Convention on the Control of Transboundary Movements of Hazardous Wastes and Their Disposal (Basel Convention). The Basel Convention aims to protect human health and the environment against the adverse effects of hazardous waste through: reducing hazardous waste generation; promoting environmentally sound management of hazardous wastes; restricting transboundary movements of hazardous wastes except where it is perceived to be in accordance with the principles of environmentally sound management; and implementing a regulatory system for permitted transboundary movements. The 14th Conference of the Parties (COP) in 2019 was a major step forward for plastic wastes under the

Basel Convention (Bodle and Sina 2019). COP-14 adopted several measures on plastic wastes, including an amendment to Annex II to bring most plastic wastes under the control of the Convention as 'other wastes' (though with some narrow exceptions). Under the Basel Convention, 'other wastes' are subject to full Basel Convention control procedures, which include Prior Informed Consent and a ban on trade in waste with non-parties. Plastic waste is now also included in Annex VIII as A3210, which means plastic waste is considered hazardous under the Convention.

Further movement is expected under the umbrella of the Basel Convention as Decision BC-14/13 of COP-14 established the mandate for a working group for a Plastic Waste Partnership to prevent and minimise the generation of plastic waste, and to improve and promote its environmentally sound management at the global, regional, and national levels. The Partnership is open to parties, non-parties, and observers, including industry observers. Its activities include undertaking capacity-building activities; analysing barriers, solutions, lessons learnt, and best practices for the prevention, minimisation, and environmentally sound management of wastes; exploring options for increasing the durability, reusability, repairability, and recyclability of plastics; and updating the Technical Guidelines for the environmentally sound management of plastic wastes.

The United Nations Environmental Assembly (UNEA), the world's highest-level decision-making body on the environment, has also acted on (circular) plastics in recent years. For example, a resolution on marine litter and microplastics was passed at the third session (UNEP/EA/3/Res.7), with another resolution on marine plastic litter and microplastics (UNEP/EA.4/Res.6) as well as a resolution on single-use plastic products (UNEP/EA.4.Res.9) at the fourth session. Moreover, the UNEA-4 Ministerial Declaration adopted at the fourth meeting in 2019 committed to 'advanc[ing] sustainable consumption and production patterns, including, but not only, through circular economy and other sustainable economic models and the implementation of the 10-Year Framework of Programmes on Sustainable Consumption and Production Patterns' and addressing 'the damage to our ecosystems caused by the unsustainable use and disposal of plastic products, including by significantly reducing the manufacturing and use of single-use plastic products by 2030, and [by working] with the private sector to find affordable and environmentally friendly alternatives' (Art. 5(b) and (l) of UNEP/EA.4HLS.1). More significantly, the fifth session adopted a resolution with a mandate to develop an international legally binding agreement on plastics pollution by 2024 (UNEP/EA.5/Res.14).[5] This resolution references the need to implement a circular plastics economy. The treaty is to include provisions '[t]o promote sustainable production and consumption of plastics through, among other things, product design and environmentally sound waste management, including through resource efficiency and circular economy approaches' (Art. 3(b)). There is also a weak call in the preamble 'to continue and step up activities, and adopt voluntary measures, to combat plastic pollution, including measures related to sustainable consumption and production, which may include circular economy approaches' (Art. 15).

A global plastics treaty is needed to facilitate coordination and global action on plastic wastes and pollution. Even though international agreements and efforts exist that address plastic pollution, such as the International Convention for the Prevention of Pollution from Ships (MARPOL Convention), the Honolulu Strategy, and the United Nations Environmental Program's Clean Seas Campaign, there are currently gaps, fragmentation, and limited coordination (Raubenheimer and McIlgorm 2017; UN Environment 2018; Bodle and Sina 2019; Environmental Investigation Agency 2021). The gaps include limited regulatory provisions on pollution from land-based sources, a focus on waste by existing rules instead of reframing for full product life cycles, and no central forum or coordinating mechanism for addressing plastic pollution issues (UN Environment 2018; Bodle and Sina 2019). Even though Art. 207 of UNCLOS requires parties to adopt measures to prevent pollution from land-based sources, including measures designed to minimise the release of harmful substances, UNCLOS does not provide for reporting, monitoring, and compliance systems. Moreover, UNCLOS does not provide guidance on implementation and assistance; its dispute settlement mechanism is adversarial and provides little incentive to use it for environmental matters; and advisory opinions have a very limited potential to provide guidance on plastics (Bodle and Sina 2019). The Basel Convention focuses on controlling transboundary movements of hazardous wastes and other wastes, and while it does address waste prevention and minimisation, it insufficiently recognises the whole life cycle of plastics (Bodle and Sina 2019). Finally, Annex V on the Prevention of Pollution by Garbage from Ships to the MARPOL Convention prohibits the discharge of all plastics at sea from ships. This was 'a great first step', but oceans have not benefited from reductions of plastic pollution since (Borrelle et al. 2017). Each of these agreements also has a particular focus (seas, transboundary movement of hazardous wastes, and ships, respectively) meaning that none can individually provide the foundation for a comprehensive international agreement on plastic wastes.

There is also a business case for a UN treaty on plastics (Nielsen et al. 2020). Nielsen et al. (2020) highlight that the current regulatory landscape for plastic pollution is inconsistent among and within countries. This means that laws are increasingly complex and costly for the private sector to navigate. The landscape is also fast-changing and unpredictable, resulting in high compliance-scanning costs. An international agreement could reduce these complexities by stabilising the legal framework and possibly standardising reporting metrics. In turn, this could facilitate better supply chain compliance with measures on plastic wastes.

A global plastics treaty should have a clear aim of a circular plastics economy with specific aims to reduce production of virgin material used in plastic production, eliminate use of harmful chemicals, and provide legislative support to stabilise and grow the recycling industry (Raubenheimer and McIlgorm 2017; Nielsen et al. 2020). This is likely to require many different measures and principles (Borrelle et al. 2017). A mix of measures should be included in an agreement on circular plastic economies, including (Borrelle et al. 2017; Bodle and Sina 2019; Nielsen et al. 2020) common definitions; harmonised regulatory standards; (inter)national goals and targets; action plans to deliver an overarching objective to prevent and mitigate plastic leakage and wastes; administrative and procedural provisions on institutions, capacity building; and common reporting metrics and methodologies. None of these measures on their own will result in the systemic shifts to CEs – there is no silver bullet – but each will contribute to providing tools and incentives for supporting CE transitions. Reporting requirements, for example, will facilitate monitoring of plastic wastes and pollution. According to Nielsen et al. (2020), currently just 39 percent of countries publicly report on waste data. Without such data, our understanding of the problem and evaluation of the effectiveness of any adopted measures is limited. Many (though not all) of these mechanisms exist at other national and subnational levels in relation to waste and in relation to particular wastes at international level (e.g., hazardous wastes covered in the Basel Convention), but also need to be part of one global, coordinated effort on plastics and plastic wastes generally.

When developing the framework for a global plastics treaty, the design should be informed by several principles and concepts we have previously referenced in this book (Borrelle et al. 2017; Center for

International Environmental Law and Environmental Investigation Agency 2018; Bodle and Sina 2019; Clift et al. 2019):

- *Life cycle of plastics*: Only considering the start of end of plastics is insufficient. Issues arise throughout the life cycle of plastics and need to be included in the problem scope.
- *Health and planetary boundaries*: Resultant actions should fit within planetary boundaries. The systems we build and materials we use need to slow climate change and reduce toxic exposure, rather than accelerate them.
- *Prevention and precaution*: We need to prevent waste. Much research remains to be done on, for example, chemical recycling and bioplastics. A preventative and precautionary approach is therefore needed.
- *Equity and justice*: Human rights to life, health, and a healthy environment must be upheld for all women, men, children, and future generations. The longevity of plastic waste affects intergenerational equity and the transboundary nature of plastics impacts intragenerational equity by affecting communities far from their point of production or consumption. This includes consideration of a just transition. The wide-ranging impacts of reduced plastics production and plastic waste generation must be recognised across all of society – both on formal and informal sectors.
- *Waste hierarchy and technical options*: Waste prevention needs to be promoted and lock-ins to reliance on continued consumption to generate wastes avoided. For example, waste-to-energy seems a short-term solution when our thinking should be for sustainable long-term transformation.
- *Multi-stakeholder participation*: The design of any international agreement on plastic pollution needs to include actors at all levels, including informal recycling workers and the sector (e.g., Ezeah et al. 2013; Velis 2021; see Section 4.3.1). The CE framework creates opportunities to make room for organised waste pickers as specialised waste management service providers (Gutberlet et al. 2017).
- *Polluter pays principle*: A polluter pays principles could be implemented through extended producer responsibility (EPR) (see Sections 2.3.2 and 3.4.1).
- *Informed choices of safer alternatives to plastics*: Research and innovative solutions as alternatives to plastics should be promoted, encouraged, and supported within the context of sustainable consumption and production pattern.

- *Counteracting practices*: Specific attention is needed to identify existing practices that 'undo' and counteract aims of agreement. Should, for example, fossil fuel subsidies be ended (Borrelle et al. 2017)?
- *Capability support*. As '[m]any regions may wish to prevent plastic emissions into the environment, but ... lack the means for waste management infrastructure' (Borrelle et al. 2017), shared access to supporting capabilities and resources such as global funds, and transfer of know-how are needed.

None of these concepts or principles are sufficient on their own, and many are even informed by others. For example, informed choices of safer alternatives to plastics should also consider the life cycles of the alternatives, as well as their impacts on health and planetary boundaries; the waste hierarchy requires implementation of the preventative approach; and equity and justice dimensions of any actions should be considered.

4.4.2 National Measures

National governance of plastic wastes is needed in addition to international governance, as often such approaches can take action more quickly. Plastic waste is a critical and time-sensitive issue – the longer we take to implement actions, the more plastics are gathering in and polluting our environments. The majority of plastic enters the ocean from a small geographic area, and over half comes from just five countries: China, Indonesia, the Philippines, Thailand, and Vietnam (Jambeck et al. 2015; Ocean Conservancy and McKinsey Center for Business and Environment 2015). Coordinated action in these five countries could reduce global plastic waste leakage by approximately 45 percent over the next ten years (Ocean Conservancy and McKinsey Center for Business and Environment 2015).

As national measures for a circular plastics economy, bans are increasingly being adopted to prevent plastic wastes. This typically includes bans on certain plastic waste imports and plastic bags. China, for example, has essentially banned imports of post-consumer and post-industrial scrap plastics; India has revised its hazardous waste rules to ban imports of solid plastic waste; Vietnam will reportedly stop accepting all scrap plastic starting in 2025; Thailand has announced it will roll out a ban on all scrap plastic imports by 2021; and Malaysia has reportedly imposed stringent controls on the import of plastic waste with a plan to ban the import of scrap plastics over the next three years. If a critical mass of countries adopts bans on plastic wastes, the resultant difficulty for moving plastic wastes around for recycling or disposal would likely disrupt other national waste collection and management schemes, necessitating a rethink of plastic wastes management more widely. Bans bring with them wider justice implications. Before a ban was introduced in Kenya, research identified an equity issue: 'Banning certain types of plastic bags, and doing awareness campaigns may be futile in the long-run in reducing consumption of plastic bags, because lack of sanitary services has forced Nairobi's poor city residents to devise other uses for plastic bags beyond those concerning shopping' (Njeru 2006). In Kenya, there were additionally concerns about procedural justice when implementing the plastic bag ban. The Kenya Association of Manufacturers criticised a lack of public participation and stakeholder consultations before the plastic bag ban was issued in the case of *Kenya Association of Manufacturers and 2 Others v Cabinet Secretary of the Ministry of Environmental and Natural Resources and 3 Others*[6] (Chore 2019).

Instead of a ban, prevention of plastics may be encouraged with variable waste charging. This instrument charges people according to the amount of plastic waste produced. In the UK, concern that variable waste charging might see a disproportionate impact on poor households were relieved somewhat by research by Dresner and Ekins (2010) that demonstrated it could be done in progressive ways where poorer households would be proportionately better off than richer households.

There is also a need to consider what the target issues of regulations are. Many current regulatory measures are not targeting the right issues. For example, in the case of national measures on single-use plastics: the EU has a Plastics Strategy (as part of which adopted the Single-Use Plastics Directive); several countries, including India, have announced commitments around eliminating single-use plastics in the coming years; the UN report that 127 countries have adopted some form of legislation regulating plastic bags, and 27 countries have enacted legislation banning other specific products, materials, or production levels; New York and California in the United States have planned plastic bags, and several other localities have taken action to ban plastic bags as well; the California legislature is considering two bills (SB 54 and AB 1080) that would require manufacturers and retailers of single-use packaging or products to reduce by 75% the waste generated from single-use packaging and products offered for sale or sold in the state through reduction, recycling or composting, in addition to other commitments. But are these measures targeting low-hanging fruits at the expense of engaging with more critical systems issues? As discussed previously, plastic bags are only part of the problem. Two-thirds of countries with legislation on plastic items regulate only single-use plastic bags, yet these bags account for only seven percent of plastic items found in beach clean-ups (Borrelle et al. 2017; Nielsen et al. 2020). Moreover, research shows that market-based measures may be insufficient for enabling circular plastic economies (Syberg et al. 2021).

Beyond national measures, local legislation can enable or hinder waste management efforts. Legislation is 'a major driver in the group of institutional drivers of waste management' as it often most directly determines the ways consumers and producers manage or dispose waste materials (Agamuthu et al. 2009). Cooperation between various national and local actors is required to ensure that laws incorporate local waste and their characteristics: '[s]ustainable waste management must be grounded in local legislation that is geographically and culturally feasible, reasonable, and far-sighted' (Agamuthu et al. 2009). At the same time, too much locally devolved autonomy over waste management could effect to a lack of action in absence of clear overarching objectives or obligations. Even where there is need and want to address waste management at the local level, there are often challenges in availability, affordability, and accessibility of financial, technical, and organisational resources required to provide the requisite services (Kosoe et al. 2019).

4.4.3 Summary

None of the top-down approaches and waste governance measures covered in this section are exclusive or necessarily specific to plastic wastes (see Section 2.3 for a general overview of the measures covered). Many are widely discussed and transferred across contexts such as bans and variable charges. Yet, this section's review of some of the international, national, and local activities and experiences in just one specific case context, that of plastic wastes, highlights that in order to meaningfully be able to engage with the justice and equity issues first discussed in broad terms in Chapter 3, the even greater diversity and complexity by which they play out in practice needs to be recognised and understood.

4.5 Conclusion

Through the case example of plastics waste, we have tried to explore some of the major governance complexities impacting CE governance. From a legal perspective, it cannot be presumed that waste is a pollutant or resource from a legal perspective. Nor is there a single, preferable legal and policy measure with which to achieve CE transitions. The comparative desirability and viability of different waste management measures and approaches depend on context. Diverse approaches that contribute towards CEs – both formal (mandated, regulatory) and informal – have been adopted by different groups in different sectors and contexts. There appears to be an often recurring two-fold pattern where top-down governance approaches draw heavily on environmental law instruments with some inclusion of economic interventions, and bottom-up approaches being led by narratives of economic cases for changes in the behaviour of waste actors.

Yet the experiences with plastic wastes suggest that radical change is not yet happening in the sector. Even when CE is claimed to be a far-reaching instrument capable of achieving radical change (see Chapter 2), the experience with plastics suggests the many challenges it faces before such beliefs will be held more widely. The continuation of consumption-supporting approaches where new resources are mined, with reuse, recycling, and recovery from waste as the focus of policies extends the linear economy status quo into the future.

Notes

1 The precise impacts on human health, however, remain unclear. More research on the impact of plastic wastes on human health is therefore needed (Davison et al. 2021).
2 See Plastic Bank. 2022. Plastic Bank. https://plasticbank.com.
3 See: Recycled Park. 2022. What is Recycled Park? www.recycledpark.com.
4 The exact genesis of waste colonialism is contested. See Liboiron (2018) and Sridhar and Kumar (2019) for brief discussions on the term's possible origins.
5 See https://unplasticstreaty.org.
6 *Kenya Association of Manufacturers and 2 Others v Cabinet Secretary of the Ministry of Environmental and Natural Resources and 3 Others* (2017) eKLR.

References

Agamuthu P., Khidzir, K.M. and Hamid, F.S. 2009. Drivers of sustainable waste management in Asia. *Waste Management and Research*, 27(7), pp.625–633. https://doi.org/10.1177/0734242X09103191.

Akpan, D.A. and Inyang, B. 2017. Economic diplomacy, global waste trade: the African perspective since the 20th century. *African Journal of History and Archaeology*, 2(1), pp.1–10.

Alliance to End Plastic Waste. 2019. The Alliance launches today. https://endplasticwaste.org/en/news/the-alliance-launches-today.

Allouzi, M.M.A., Tang, D.Y.Y., Chew, K.W., Rinklebe, J., Bolan, N., Allouzi, S.F. and Show, P.L. 2021. Micro (nano) plastic pollution: the ecological influence on soil-plant system and human health. *Science of the Total Environment*, 788, p.147815. https://doi.org/10.1016/j.scitotenv.2021.147815.

Bening, C.R., Kahlert, S. and Asiedu, E. 2022. The true cost of solving the plastic waste challenge in developing countries: the case of Ghana. *Journal of Cleaner Production*, 330, p.129649. https://doi.org/10.1016/j.jclepro.2021.129649.

Bodle, R. and Sina, S. 2019. *A Treaty on Plastic Waste.* Discussion paper. Eco logic. www.muell-im-meer.de/sites/default/files/2019-12/2588-treaty-plastic-draft_discussion_paper.pdf.

Borrelle, S.B., Rochman, C.M., Liboiron, M., Bond, A.L., Lusher, A., Bradshaw, H. and Provencher, J.F. 2017. Why we need an international agreement on marine plastic pollution. *PNAS*, 114(38), pp.9994–9997. https://doi.org/10.1073/pnas.1714450114.

Burlakovs, J., Kriipsalu, M., Klavins, M., Bhatnagar, A., Vincevica-Gaile, Z., Stenis, J., Jani, Y., Mykhaylenko, V., Denafas, G., Turkadze, T., Hogland, M., Rudovica, V., Kaczala, F., Rosendal, R.M. and Hogland, W. 2017. Paradigms on landfill mining: from dump site scavenging to ecosystem services revitalization. *Resources, Conservation and Recycling*, 123, pp.73–84. https://doi.org/10.1016/j.resconrec.2016.07.007.

Byung-wook, K. 2021. Korea District Heating Corp. pledges to turn plastic waste into hydrogen. *The Korea Herald.* www.koreaherald.com/view.php?ud=20210623000897.

Center for International Environmental Law and Environmental Investigation Agency. 2018. Joint position statement: first meeting of the ad hoc open-ended expert group on marine litter and microplastics. 1st AHOEEG Meeting (May 2018).

Chertow, M. 2007. "Uncovering" industrial symbiosis. *Journal of Industrial Ecology*, 11(1), pp.11–30. https://doi.org/10.1162/jiec.2007.1110.

Chore, T. 2019. Reconceptualising the right to a clean and healthy environment in Kenya: The need to move from an anthropocentric view to a bicentric view. *Strathmore Law Review*, 4, pp.71–89.

Clift, R., Baumann, H., Murphy, R.J. and Stahel, W.R. 2019. Making plastics: uses, losses and disposal. *Law Environment and Development Journal*, 15(2), pp.93–107. https://doi.org/10.25501/SOAS.00033067.

Cook, E. and Velis, C.A. 2020. *Global Review on Safer End of Engineered Life.* Royal Academy of Engineering and the Lloyd's Register Foundation. Royal Academy of Engineering. p.60. www.raeng.org.uk/global/international-partnerships/engineering-x-old/safer-end-engineered-life/global-review-on-safer-end-of-engineered-life.

Corvellec, H., Campos, M.J.Z. and Zapata, P. 2013. Infrastructures, lock-in, and sustainable urban development: the case of waste incineration in the Göteborg Metropolitan Area. *Journal of Cleaner Production*, 50, pp.32–39. https://doi.org/10.1016/j.jclepro.2012.12.009.

Davison, S.M.C., White, M.P., Pahl, S., Taylor, T., Fielding, K., Roberts, B.R., Economou, T., McMeel, O., Kellett, P. and Fleming, L.E. 2021 Public concern about, and desire for research into, the human health effects of marine plastic pollution: results from a 15-country survey across Europe and Australia. *Global Environmental Change*, 69, p.102309. https://doi. org/10.1016/j.gloenvcha.2021.102309.

Dong, L., Zhang, H., Fujita, T., Ohnishi, S., Li, H., Fujii, M. and Dong, H. 2013. Environmental and economic gains of industrial symbiosis for Chinese iron/steel industry: Kawasaki's experience and practice in Liuzhou and Jinan. *Journal of Cleaner Production*, 59, pp.226–238. https://doi. org/10.1016/j.jclepro.2013.06.048.

Dresner, S. and Ekins, P. 2010. Charging for domestic waste in England: combining environmental and equity considerations. *Resources Conservation and Recycling*, 54(12), pp.1100–1108. https://doi.org/10.1016/j. resconrec.2010.03.001.

Emadian, S.M., Onay, T.T. and Demirel, B. 2017. Biodegradation of bioplastics in natural environments. *Waste Management*, 59, pp.526–536. https:// doi.org/10.1016/j.wasman.2016.10.006.

Environmental Investigation Agency. 2021. *The Truth Behind Trash. The Scale and Impact of the International Trade in Plastic Waste.* https://eia-international.org/report/the-truth-behind-trash-the-scale-and-impact-of-the-international-trade-in-plastic-waste/.

Eun, J.-J. 2021. Hyundai Engineering to make hydrogen from plastic waste. *The Korea Economic Daily.* www.kedglobal.com/plastic-recycling/newsView/ked202112220005.

Ezeah, C., Fazakerley, J.A. and Roberts, C.L. 2012. Emerging trends in informal sector recycling in developing and transition countries. *Waste Management*, 33(11), pp.2509–2519. https://doi.org/10.1016/j.wasman.2013.06.020.

Garcia, J.M. and Robertson, M.L. 2017. The future of plastics recycling. *Science*, 358(6365), pp.870–872. https://doi.org/10.1126/science.aaq0324.

Geyer, R., Jambeck, J.R. and Law, K.L. 2017. Production, use, and fate of all plastics ever made. *Science Advances*, 3(7). https://doi.org/10.1126/sciadv.17007.

Goldstein, J. 2016. A pyrrhic victory? The limits to the successful crackdown on informal-sector plastics recycling in Wenan County, China. *Modern China*, 43(1), pp.3–35.

Gunsilius, E., Spies, S., Garcia-Cortes, S., Medina, M., Dias, S., Scheinberg, A., Sabry, W., Abdel-Hady, N., Florisbela dos Santas, A.-L. and Ruis, S. 2011. *Recovering Resources, Creating Opportunities: Integrating the Informal Sector into Solid Waste Management.* GIZ. www.giz.de/en/downloads/giz2011-en-recycling-partnerships-informal-sector-final-report.pdf.

Gutberlet, J. and Baeder, A.M. 2008. Informal recycling and occupational health in Santo André, Brazil. *International Journal of Environmental Health Research*, 18(1), pp.1–15. https://doi.org/10.1080/09603120701844258.

Gutberlet, J., Carenzo, S., Kain, J.-H. and de Azevedo, A.M.M. 2017. Waste picker organizations and their contribution to the circular economy. Two case studies from a Global South perspective. *Resources*, 6(4), p.52. https://doi.org/10.3390/resources6040052.

Hashimoto, S., Fujita, T., Geng, Y. and Nagasawa, E. 2010. Realizing CO2 emission reduction through industrial symbiosis: a cement production case study for Kawasaki. *Resources, Conservation and Recycling*, 54(10), pp.704–710. https://doi.org/10.1016/j.resconrec.2009.11.013.

He, Z., Li, G., Chen, J., Huang, Y., An, T. and Zhang, C. 2015. Pollution characteristics and health risk assessment of volatile organic compounds emitted from different plastic solid waste recycling workshops. *Environment International*, 77, pp.85–94. https://doi.org/10.1016/j.envint.2015.01.004.

Jambeck, J.R., Geyer, R., Wilcox, C. Siegler, T.R., Perryman, M., Andrady, A., Narayan, R. and Law, K.L. 2015. Plastic waste inputs from land into the ocean. *Science*, 347(6223), pp.768–771. https://doi.org/10.1126/science.1260352.

Jie, X., Li, W., Slocombe, D. et al. 2020. Microwave-initiated catalytic deconstruction of plastic waste into hydrogen and high-value carbons. *Nature Catalysis* 3, pp.902–912. https://doi.org/10.1038/s41929-020-00518-5.

Kosoe, E.A., Diawuo, F. and Osumanu, I.K. 2019. Looking into the past: rethinking traditional ways of solid waste management in the Jaman South municipality, Ghana. *Ghana Journal of Geography*, 11(1), pp.228–244. https://doi.org/10.4314/gjg.v11i1.13.

Krivtsov, V., Wäger, P.A., Dacombe, P., Gilgen, P.W., Heaven, S., Hilty, L.M. and Banks, C.J. 2004. Analysis of energy footprints associated with recycling of glass and plastic—case studies for industrial ecology. *Ecological Modelling*, 174(1–2), pp.175–189. https://doi.org/10.1016/j.ecolmodel.2004.01.007.

Kunzig, R. 2020. Let's not waste this crucial moment: we need to stop abusing the planet. *National Geographic.* www.nationalgeographic.com/magazine/article/lets-not-waste-this-crucial-moment-we-need-to-stop-abusing-the-planet-feature.

Lau, W., Shiran, Y., Bailey, R.M. et al. 2020. Evaluating scenarios toward zero plastic pollution. *Science*, 369(6510), pp.1455–1461. https://doi.org/10.1126/science.aba9475.

Lausselet C., Cherubini, F., Oreggioni, G.B., Serrano, G.d.A., Becidan, M., Hu, X., Rørstad, P.K. and Strømman, A.H. 2017. Norwegian waste-to-energy: climate change, circular economy and carbon capture and storage. *Resources, Conservation and Recycling*, 126, pp.50–61. https://doi.org/10.1016/j.resconrec.2017.07.025.

Liboiron. 2018. *Waste Colonialism.* https://discardstudies.com/2018/11/01/waste-colonialism/.

Mahabir, S., Jagassar, I., Millette, S., Andrade, J., Boodoo, G., Garcia, A., Parasram-Andrade, A. and Andrade, J. 2020. *Industrial Symbiosis (IS) in Plastics: a Caribbean Cluster-based Case for a Viable Caribbean Circular Economy.* CWWA 29th Annual Conference and Exhibition. Water Security and Waste Reduction Sustainability in Uncertain Times. www.undp.org/

sites/g/files/zskgke326/files/migration/tt/Industrial-Symbiosis-in-Plastics---CWWA-2020.pdf.

Merrington, A. 2017. Recycling of plastics. In: *Applied Plastic Engineering Handbook*, 2nd ed, pp.167–189. https://doi.org/10.1016/B978-0-323-39040-8.00009-2.

Midili, A., Kucuk, H., Haciosmanoglu, M., Akbulut, U. and Dincer, I. 2021. A review on converting plastic wastes into clean hydrogen via gasification for better sustainability. *International Journal of Energy Research*, 46(4), pp.4001–4032. https://doi.org/10.1002/er.7498.

Mulholland, K.L. and Dyer, J.A. 1999. *Pollution Prevention: Methodology, Technologies and Practices*. American Institute of Chemical Engineers.

Narancic, T., O'Connor, K.E. 2019. Plastic waste as a global challenge: are biodegradable plastics the answer to the plastic waste problem? *Microbiology*, 165(2), pp.129–137. https://doi.org/10.1099/mic.0.000749.

Nielsen, J., Unnikrishnan, S., Portfaix, A. and Cottee-Jones, E. 2020. *We Need a Global Agreement to Address Plastic Pollution*. Accessed 16 February 2021. www.bcg.com/en-gb/publications/2020/global-agreement-to-address-plastic-pollution.

Njeru, J. 2006. The urban political ecology of plastic bag waste problem in Nairobi, Kenya. *Geoforum*, 37(6), pp.1046–1058. https://doi.org/10.3390/resources6040052.

North, E.J. and Halden, R.U. 2013. Plastics and environmental health: the road ahead. *Reviews on Environmental Health*. https://doi.org/10.1515/reveh-2012-0030.

Ocean Conservancy and McKinsey Center for Business and Environment. 2015. *Stemming the Tide: Land-based Strategies for a Plastic-free Ocean*. www.mckinsey.com/business-functions/sustainability/our-insights/saving-the-ocean-from-plastic-waste.

Ogwueleke, T.C. and BP, N. 2021. Activities of informal recycling sector in North-Central, Nigeria. *Energy Nexus*, 1, p.100003. https://doi.org/10.1016/j.nexus.2021.100003.

Ojeda-Benitez, S., Armijo-de-Vega, C. and Ramirez-Barreto, M.E. 2002. Formal and informal recovery of recyclables in Mexicali, Mexico: handling alternatives. *Resources, Conservation and Recycling*, 34(4), pp.273–288.

Oyegunle, A. and Thompson, S. 2018. Wasting indigenous communities: A case study with Garden Hill and Wasagamack First Nations in Northern Manitoba, Canada. *The Journal of Solid Waste Technology and Management*, 44(3), pp.232–247. https://doi.org/10.5276/JSWTM.2018.232.

Parker, L. 2018. Here's how much plastic trash is littering the Earth. *National Geographic* www.nationalgeographic.com/news/2017/07/plastic-produced-recycling-waste-ocean-trash-debris-environment/.

Parker, L. 2020. An old-school plan to fight plastic pollution gathers steam. *National Geographic*. www.nationalgeographic.com/science/article/old-school-plan-to-fight-plastic-pollution-gathers-steam.

Payne, J. and Jones, M.D. 2021. The chemical recycling of polyesters for a circular plastics economy: challenges and emerging opportunities. *ChemSusChem*, 14(19), pp.4041–4070. https://doi.org/10.1002/cssc. 202100400.

Penteado, C.S.G. and de Castro, M.A.S. 2021. Covid-19 effects on municipal solid waste management: what can effectively be done in the Brazilian scenario? *Resources Conservation and Recycling*, 164, pp.1–9. https://doi. org/10.1016/j.resconrec.2020.105152.

Pew Charitable Trusts and SYSTEMIQ. 2020. *Breaking the Plastic Wave: A Comprehensive Assessment of Pathways Towards Stopping Ocean Plastic Pollution.* www.pewtrusts.org/-/media/assets/2020/10/breakingtheplasticwave_mainreport.pdf.

Plastic Bank. 2022. *Plastic Bank.* https://plasticbank.com.

Rahimi, A. and García, J. 2017. Chemical recycling of waste plastics for new materials production. *Nature Reviews Chemistry*, 1, p.0046. https://doi. org/10.1038/s41570-017-0046.

Raubenheimer, K. and McIlgorm, A. 2017. Is the Montreal Protocol a model that can help solve the global plastic debris problem? *Marine Policy*, 81, pp.322–329. https://doi.org/10.1016/j.marpol.2017.04.014.

Rochman, C.M., Browne, M.A., Underwood, A.J., van Franeker, J.A., Thompson, R.C. and Amaral-Zettler, L.A. 2016. The ecological impacts of marine debris: unraveling the demonstrated evidence from what is perceived. *Ecology*, 97(2), pp.302–312. https://doi.org/10.1890/14-2070.1.

Schneider, P., Anh, L.H., Wagner, J., Reichenbach, J. and Hebner, A. 2017. Solid waste management in Ho Chi Minh City, Vietnam: moving towards a circular economy? *Sustainability*, 9(2), p.286. https://doi.org/10.3390/su9020286.

Siragusa, L. and Arzyutov, D. 2020. Nothing goes to waste: sustainable practices of re-use among indigenous groups in the Russian North. *Current Opinion in Environmental Sustainability*, 43, pp.41–48. https://doi. org/10.1016/j.cosust.2020.02.001.

Springer, A.L. 1977. Towards a meaningful concept of pollution in international law. *The International and Comparative Law Quarterly*, 26(3), pp.531–557.

Sridhar, L. and Kumar, P. 2019. The new face of waste colonialism: a review of legal regulations governing the import of waste into India. *Socio-Legal Review*, 15(2), pp.101–130.

Steenmans, K., Taylor, P. and Steenmans, I. 2021. Blockchain technology for governance of plastic waste management: where are we? *Social Sciences*, 10(11), 434. https://doi.org/10.3390/socsci10110434.

Syberg, K., Nielsen, M.B., Clausen, L.P.W., van Calster, G., van Wazel, A., Rochman, C., Koelmans, A.A., Cronin, R., Pahl, S. and Hansen, S.F. 2021. Regulation of plastic from a circular economy perspective. *Current Opinion in Green and Sustainable Chemistry*, 29, p.100462. https://doi.org/10.1016/j. cogsc.2021.100462.

Tabone, M.D., Cregg, J.J., Beckman, E.J. and Landis, A.E. 2010.Sustianability metrics: life cycle assessment and green design in polymers. *Environmental Science and Technology*, 44, pp.8264–8269. https://doi.org/10.1021/es101640n.

UN Environment Programme. 2018. *Combating Marine Plastic Litter and Microplastics: An Assessment of the Effectiveness of Relevant International, Regional and Subregional Governance Strategies and Approaches.* 15 February 2018. UNEP/EA.3/INF/5.

UNPRI. 2019. *The Plastics Landscape: The Challenges and Possible Solutions.* www.unpri.org/download?ac=7014.

Upham, P. and Jones, C. 2012. Don't lock me in: public opinion on the prospective use of waste process heating for district heating. *Applied Energy*, 89(1), pp.21–29. https://doi.org/10.1016/j.apenergy.2011.02.031.

Van Heijnsbergen, P. 1979. The pollution concept in international law. *Environmental Policy and Law*, 5(1), pp.11–13.

Velis, C.A. 2021. Plastic pollution global treaty to cover waste pickers and open burning. *Waste Management & Research: The Journal for a Sustainable Circular Economy*, 40(1), pp.1–2. https://doi.org/10.1177/0734242X211069583.

Wagner-Lawlor, J. 2018. Poor theory and the art of plastic pollution in Nigeria: relational aesthetics, human ecology, and "good housekeeping". *Social Dynamics: A Journal of African Studies*, 44(2), pp.198–220. https://doi.org/10.1080/02533952.2018.1481685.

Waluda, C.M. and Staniland, I.J. 2013. Entanglement of Antarctic fur seals at Bird Island, South Georgia. *Marine Pollution Bulletin*, 74, pp.244–252. https://doi.org/10.1016/j.marpolbul.2013.06.050.

Westlake, K. 1995. *Landfill Waste Pollution and Control.* Cambridge: Woodhead Publishing.

White, A. and Lockyer, S. 2020. Removing plastic packaging from fresh produce – what's the impact? *Nutrition Bulletin*, 45(1), pp.35–50. https://doi.org/10.1111/nbu.12420.

Wilson, D.C., Velis, C. and Cheeseman, C. 2006. Role of informal sector recycling in waste management in developing countries. *Habitat International*, 30(4), pp.797–808. https://doi.org/10.1016/j.habitatint.2005.09.005.

Wuyts, W., Marin, J., Brusselaers, J. and Vrancken, K. 2020. Circular economy as a COVID-19 cure? *Resources, Conservation and Recycling*, 162, p.105016. https://doi.org/10.1016/j.resconrec.2020.105016.

Yang, H., Ma, M., Thompson, J.R. and Flower, R.J. 2018. Waste management, informal recycling, environmental pollution and public health. *Journal of Epidemiology and Community Health*, 72 (3). pp.237–243. https://doi.org/10.1136/jech-2016-208597.

5 Circular Bioeconomy and Forests

As with other circular economy (CE) sectors from textiles to steel to plastics, the circular forest bioeconomy (CFBE) is in its early stages. Although certain CFBE aspects, such as packaging and paper recycling, biomass from forest residues, and forest carbon markets, already exist, an integrated circular system has yet to be established that cascades materials from across the sector within a maximum value closed loop in accordance with CE principles. Currently, the CFBE is an amalgam of contested, often imprecise, concepts and definitions. We argue that law and policy-makers need to adopt a critical approach to how the CFBE is framed and explore the implications differing constructs might have on justice outcomes, especially for forest-dependent and indigenous peoples, biodiversity, and related ecosystems.

5.1 Introduction

The scale of anthropogenic forest resource extraction and processing with its complex feedback loops to ecosystem degradation, including soil and hydrological functions, species habitat destruction, and climate change, are well documented (see IPBES 2019). The associated interlinkages between ecosystem degradation and poverty, food insecurity, as well as more extensive human and indigenous rights abuses are equally well recognised (see Millennium Ecosystem Assessment 2005). In 1948, the first UN Food and Agricultural Organization's Forest Resources Assessment highlighted problems associated with deforestation including the negative impact for food security, human livelihoods, and biodiversity (Garzuglia 2018). Between 2001 and 2020, there was a ten percent decrease in tree cover globally resulting in loss of biodiverse-rich habitats, especially in tropical regions (Global Forest Watch 2020). By 2018, a UNEP-IRP report stated that

DOI: 10.4324/9780429355141-5

extraction and processing of land-based resources collectively was directly associated with 50 percent of all human impact on the climate and 90 percent of all biodiversity loss and water stress (UNEP-IRP 2019). Forestry and forest land clearance for agroindustry are significant drivers behind the ecological destruction and its impacts. For example, combined they contribute approximately 23 percent of total greenhouse gas emissions globally (IPCC 2019).

New forest management concepts have been tried by many countries and transnational organisations over numerous decades to tackle deforestation and degradation, and the associated environmental and social impacts. In the early 1990s–2000s, voluntary market-based certification schemes, such as the Forest Stewardship Council (FSC) and the Programme for the Endorsement of Forest Certification, were developed to drive sustainable forest management practices. Meanwhile under the 1992 UN Framework Convention on Climate Change's (UNFCCC) Kyoto Protocol (1998), new forest carbon trading markets were created to place a value on standing forests ecosystem sequestration capacity. By the 2010s countries around the world began adopting bioeconomy (BE) strategies and plans, including United States' Bioeconomy Blueprint (2012), South Africa's Bioeconomy Strategy (2013), Finland's National Bioeconomy Strategy (2014), and Canada's Forest Bioeconomy Framework (2017), to promote a more integrated business model approach to the forest sector. Increasingly, the BE became associated and/or incorporated into CE plans and policies and vice versa. For example, in 2018, the EU incorporated the CE into its BE definition in a revision to the 2012 European Bioeconomy Strategy. The term circular forest bioeconomy (CFBE) began to gain traction. The move to adopt CE as a frame reflects a wider shift towards incorporating CE principles into all economic sectors by many countries. The CFBE promises to be able to achieve what the modern industrial scale approach has failed to deliver, which is a sustainable forest business model that benefits all stakeholders including forest-dependent peoples, biodiversity, and related ecosystems.

In Section 5.2, competing BE and circular bioeconomy (CBE) definitions are set out, and the implications these have when applied specifically to forests is considered. Section 5.3 provides an introductory overview to the historical and political economic context of forest resource extraction management and related laws. In the section, the interlinkages with current law and forest approaches that continue to perpetuate long-standing inequity and injustices, especially for marginalised forest communities and indigenous peoples, are surveyed.

Also, emerging trends in law that could potentially lead to a paradigm shift in how natural resources are valued, are discussed. Finally, Section 5.4 focuses on two examples within the forest resource sector that are associated with achieving a CFBE. Through the case studies: forest carbon sequestration services and bioenergy we highlight the tensions between sustainability, waste definitions, climate change, property/land law, and indigenous peoples' rights for the CFBE. In conclusion, we argue that the CFBE will not be able to deliver sustainable circularity nor on long overdue justice promises, if it continues to pursue current law and policy measures.

5.2 Concept and Definitions

The CFBE is an amalgam of contested, often imprecise, concepts and definitions. Like the CE there is no single BE definition, similarly there is no universal legal forest definition. Definitions employed by policy-makers, law-makers, and other key stakeholders for a CFBE by transnational organisations, businesses, civil society, and forest-based indigenous communities, already vary. This section highlights how BE definitions have evolved and incorporated both the CE concept and particular forest definitions.

5.2.1 Bioeconomy

A BE remains an evolving, ambiguous, and contested concept with multiple definitions and delimitations to its scope. It is by nature intersectoral, (inter)national, and transdisciplinary and operates within multiple spatial and temporal scales (Mittra and Zoukas 2020; Barañano et al. 2021; Kardung et al. 2021). The concept's origins lie with Russian biologist F.I. Baranoff who coined the term 'bioeconomics' in the 1930s (see Kardung et al. 2021). Baranoff combined the disciplines of ecology and economics to apply them to fisheries resource management, developing the concept of maximum sustainable yield. In 1975, economist Georgescu-Roegen (1975) expanded the bioeconomic concept's scope by recognising its potential to be applied at a planetary scale. For Georgescu-Roegen bioeconomics could be applied to the problem of how to 'replace high-density low entropy fossil sources' such as coal, oil, and gas, the energy that powered human activities within the dominant global western modern economic system since the industrial revolution. Georgescu-Roegen's proposed solution was to create a 'minimal bioeconomic' world programme that was based on sufficiency, degrowth, and zero waste within the Earth's bio-agricultural systems carrying capacity (Georgescu-Roegen 1975). As the concept has become increasingly prominent on the global agenda BE definitions delimiting the scope and approaches have been developed by academics, organisations, and governments (Mittra and Zoukas 2020).

The OECD, an early advocate of the BE, proposed that it is constituted by three elements: biotechnological knowledge, renewable biomass, and integration across applications including agriculture and forestry (OECD 2009). In 2018, the International Advisory Council at the Global Bioeconomy Summit adopted the BE definition as 'the production, utilization, conservation, and regeneration of biological resources, including related knowledge, science, technology, and innovation, to provide sustainable solutions (information, products, processes, and services) within and across all economic sectors and enable a transformation to a sustainable economy' (International Advisory Council on Global Bioeconomy 2020). While the EU adopted a more expansive interpretation claiming that 'the bioeconomy covers all sectors and systems that rely on biological resources (animals, plants, micro-organisms and derived biomass, including organic waste), their functions and principles. It includes and interlinks land and marine ecosystems and the services they provide; all primary production sectors that use and produce biological resources (agriculture, forestry, fisheries, and aquaculture); and all economic and industrial sectors that use biological resources and processes to produce food, feed, bio-based products, energy, and services' (European Commission 2018). Kardung et al. (2021) classified the BE as natural resource-based activities that directly exploit bioresources (agriculture, fishery, forestry) and provide biomass for further processing; conventional manufacturing activities that further process biomass (food sector, wood processing sector); and novel activities that further process the biomass and/or biomass residues (bioenergy sector, bio-based chemical sector). Although there is similarity with Georgescu-Roegen's framing, no mention is made of degrowth or sufficiency by Kardung et al. This is not uncommon as we shall see, the BE as with the CE, is frequently associated with promissory sustainable development and green growth economic systems.

Despite different definitions and emphasis, there appears to be a consensus amongst advocates that a BE refers to the sustainable use of renewable biological resources and organic wastes to produce food, feed, bio-based products, and bioenergy (Barañano et al. 2021).

Vivien et al. (2019) argue that there is an assumption that attaching the prefix "bio" to the term "economy" will bring economics and ecology together to achieve sustainable development as Baranoff originally intended. However, sustainable outcomes are by no means guaranteed in any BE. As Barañano et al. (2021) observe depending on how 'the bioeconomy transition [is pursued it] may either address fossil fuel dependence sustainably or aggravate human pressure on the environment'. For instance, Bastos Lima and Palme (2021) argue that 'corporate agribusiness dominance [already] limits the bioeconomy agenda'. In reality, multiple governance factors, including law and policy framing, will determine whether a strong or weak sustainable BE is realised (Liobikiene et al. 2019; Deciancio et al. 2022). There are multiple pathways to establish a BE, many of which are yet to be explored or exploited (Gawel et al. 2019; D'Adamo et al. 2022; Stark et al. 2022). By incorporating CE principles, some believe a more sustainable outcome for a CFBE is achievable. In 2018, the EU revised its BE strategy stressing that 'to be successful, the European bioeconomy needs to have sustainability and circularity at its heart' (European Commission 2018). So, what does it mean to incorporate CE principles into the BE? In the next section, we examine and consider the implications of merging the concepts of CE and BE.

5.2.2 *Merging with the Circular Economy*

In 2017, the Argentinian Bioeconomia strategy specifically placed BE development within the CE (Bisang and Trigo 2018). The EU subsequently in 2018 incorporated the CE into its BE definition when it revised its 2012 European Bioeconomy Strategy (European Commission 2018). D'Amato et al. (2019) claim that although both 'circular bioeconomy and bioeconomy are conceptually distinct from one another they essentially promulgate and profess' the same goals. We argue, however, that combining CE into the BE adds new dimensions and layers to already contested concepts, which will have implications for how law and policy across sectors are designed and implemented.

A core concept behind the CBE is the distinction between the technical and biological cycles. The Ellen MacArthur Foundation (EMF) distinguishes between 'technical cycles [in which] priorities are recovering and restoring products, components and materials through strategies such as reuse, repair, remanufacture or, in the last resort, recycling [and] biological cycles [that] place the emphasis on cascading bio-based materials where they are recycled back into manufacturing processes until reaching an end point where they are used for regenerative soil improvement' (EMF 2022). The distinction between technical and biological fits with the Centre for International Forestry Research (CIFOR) CBE as an 'economy powered by nature...a new economic model that emphasizes the use of renewable natural capital and focuses on minimizing waste, replacing the wide range of non-renewable, fossil-based products currently in use' (CIFOR 2021). While Stegmann et al. (2020) set out CBE's main objective as the 'sourcing of sustainable biomass, durable and circular product design, usage of waste and residues, biofuels and bioenergy, bio-based products, food and feed, extended and shared use, composting and recovering of energy, along with recycling and cascading use' (see Khan and Ali 2022). At its simplest, using a framing around biological cycles, a CBE is characterised by biofuels and biomaterials as input and recyclable products as outputs. As Brandão et al. (2021) argue 'to guarantee circularity, the process must operate according to a cascading model (i) biomass (generated from solar energy) is converted into products; (ii) the waste stream of this process is used as a supply stream for a lower-level production process; (iii) this latter process is repeated until the waste stream can no longer be transformed into products; and (iv) waste is incinerated to provide energy to different steps within the closed loop. In this way, [BE] should be the epitome of the "zero-waste" goal'. The framing for the CBE appears aligned with Georgescu-Roegen's expanded bioeconomic concept which he set out in 1975.

A fundamental challenge though for both CE and BE concepts is that neither can be achieved through solely either the technical or the biological spheres (Carus and Dammer 2018; Cullen 2017). CIFOR clearly places an emphasis on the need for technological interventions to achieve the CBE end goals in 'sectors like forestry [where there is a need to] work in an intentionally crafted, circular manner, with scientific approaches and technological innovations employed to create more sustainable materials and spur regeneration' (CIFOR 2021). In our case studies, we show how the artificial separation between the technical and biological cycles can result in misleading claims about the CBFE, and the development of laws and policies to advance it. Before doing so we will conclude this section by examining how forest definitions used within the CBFE can have a determining effect on the outcomes promised in policy, especially regarding the 2015 Sustainable Development Goals (SDGs).

5.2.3 *Incorporating Forests*

Both BE and CFBE are anticipated by advocates to deliver enormous, unprecedented benefits and solutions to forests ecosystems, forest communities and help address global challenges like climate change and biodiversity loss. The Confederation of European Forest Owners claims the BE 'will boost the potential of the forest sector to deliver solutions to multiple challenges [including] achieving [SDGs], for example, by providing climate action, sustaining life on land, delivering work and economic growth, enhancing responsible production and consumption, boosting industry innovation and infrastructure, creating sustainable cities and communities, enhancing good health and well-being, and providing clean energy' (CEFO 2017). A CFBE is viewed as an opportunity to add value to forest-based resource materials. CIFOR proposes that 'our economic system has failed to value nature [and that a] circular bioeconomy offers a solution'. It is estimated that CFBE has a potential promissory value globally of approximately USD 3.5 trillion in business opportunities and 87 million jobs by 2030 (CIFOR 2021).

It is common in the forestry sector, as it is for other sectors, for new development and managerial approaches to have significant promissory value associated with them. The potential financial opportunities identified provide justification for policy change and subsequent laws and regulations to advance the new approach (Lesniewska 2019). As Chapter 1 outlined this is also the case with the CE. A caveat will often be included to caution stakeholders that a particular method must be adopted for the new approach to work. For example, the EU Commission stated that a holistic assessment and system-perspective are required if benefits from a CFBE are to be realised (Grassi et al. 2021). The scope for a systemic transformation within a CFBE requires alignment, including forest definitions used within law and policy.

Forest definitions have a determining impact on the design and scope for law and policy areas such as harvesting, bioenergy, biodiversity conservation, and forest carbon sequestration management, especially when it comes to issues such as access, user rights, and sustainability (Van Noordwijk and Minang 2009). Definitions have implications for how forest activities' criteria and metrics are determined, monitored, assessed, and evaluated (Chazdon et al. 2016). There is no consensus at any governance level, be that international, regional, national, or even local in some jurisdictions, over how a forest should be defined (Lund 2002). As such forests are not defined within any CFBE definition. However, despite there being hundreds of forest definitions globally contained in law, as well as unrecognised indigenous forest peoples' customary definitions, one international treaty definition has come to dominate forest-related law and policy globally in recent years (Sasaki and Putz 2009).

The 1992 UNFCCC has had a significant impact on how forests and forest activities are defined, monitored, and quantified (Trines et al. 2006). The UNFCCC definition includes plantations as forests, permits a minimum tree height of 2 m at maturity and also allows areas deforested 'as a result of human intervention such as harvesting or natural causes but which are expected to revert to forest' to be counted as forest. There is no requirement to specify when restoration of the deforested areas must be completed.[1] The UNFCCC definition contrasts with that used by the Convention on Biological Diversity (CBD). The CBD definition focuses on the forest quality, including biodiversity and ecosystems health, and excludes plantations. Deforested areas are not included regardless of whether there is an intention to reforest at an unspecified future date.[2]

The UNFCCC's forest definition was designed for forest-related policies in the Kyoto Protocol and subsequently adopted to be used for the mechanisms to reduce emissions from deforestation and degradation (REDD+), which was included in Art. 5 of the 2015 Paris Agreement. The UNFCCC's forest definition has informed CFBE-related activities through parties' national climate change strategies submitted under the Paris Agreement, referred to as Nationally Determined Contributions.[3] Just how key forest definitions are to the success or failure of policies associated with the concept of a CFBE, and whether they contribute to an equitable and just one, will be discussed in the following sections.

5.2.4 Summary

The CBE is a novel concept we are seeing increasingly used in reference to forests. The divergence in conceptual definitions of both BE and CBE causes uncertainty, vagueness, and unpredictability as to what exactly CBFE aims to achieve and how. The dominance of powerful actors (both states and business), and influential international legal regimes such as climate change, are already having a determining impact on the framing of laws and policy for the CBFE. The top-down approach continues a well-established pattern of external actors and forest governance that does not recognise indigenous peoples and forest communities' traditional knowledge and values as equally significant.

5.3 Forest Law Issues

The CFBE is being built on the foundation of laws, both public and private, that are already in place. Laws relating to forest access, use, harvesting, and trade collectively make up a fragmented transnational, polycentric multilevel regime (Arts et al. 2010; Giessen 2013). New forest resource laws and policies which fail to understand historical and current equity and justice issues within established ones have in the past led to tensions, divisions, and conflict amongst forest stakeholders especially between governments, businesses, forest-dependent communities, and indigenous peoples (Lesniewska 2016). This section focuses on selected issues, past as well as present, of forest-related laws.

5.3.1 Forest-Related Laws' Roots

Diverse forest resource extraction laws have existed throughout the world for thousands of years, dominated by customary and community-based approaches. The allocation of access, user and harvesting rights to forest ecosystems were often more respectful of biological rhythms, working within natural limits (Williams 2003). It was not until the industrial revolution in Europe in the late 18th century that the legal transformations necessary for a take-make-dispose linear forestry economic approach took root and spread around the world. The industrial revolution ushered in a natural resource capital-intensive economic model that consumed resources (human and natural) at unsustainable volumes at a pace and density greater than the Earth can provide, and forests were no exception (Galaz et al. 2012; Giampietro 2019).

The industrial revolution in Europe and settler colonies in the United States, Canada, and Australia was accompanied by a parallel transplant of legal systems, including colonised countries like India (Parfitt 2019). Legal transplants transformed how forest ecosystems were valued from being the primary source of food, water, medicines, shelter, and spiritual culture for a significant proportion of the world's human land-based communities to a resource that was controlled by a minority of non-forest dwellers (Barton 2001). The epistemological division between nature and (human) culture provided justification for devaluing forest ecosystems to a mere resource to be appropriated, extracted, processed, and consumed, which was reflected in newly adopted natural resource laws (Moore 2015; Foster and Clark 2020). From this point, the legal tools: investment, contract, and property rights (including intellectual property rights) have been systematically incorporated into all areas of sovereign statutory and international law, both public and private, so an individual owner, either a state or a transnational business, can appropriate forest resources to extract and trade them as a commodity through an ever-increasingly global market. Today most forest resource rights holders through ownership or long-term concession contracts, in former colonial countries, are either, private multinational enterprises with CEOs located in capital cities in countries far from the forest itself or state governments (White and Martin 2002; Rights and Resources Initiative 2015). One significant consequence of this is that forest communities and indigenous peoples frequently find themselves on the wrong side of the law as self-determination, customary access rights, and user rights are frequently criminalised (Tacconi et al. 2003).

The pattern of forest ecosystems' resource appropriation, especially in the Global South, has continued in the 21st century through international law initiatives to address climate change and biodiversity loss (Hahn et al. 2015). The use of legal mechanisms such as contracts, property rights supported by civil and criminal laws have enclosed ecosystem services to create new tradable commodities on global markets most notably forest carbon sequestration (Fairhead et al. 2012). The drive to value standing forests has overall had a perverse impact on forest-dependent communities and indigenous peoples. As our case studies on forest carbon trading and bioenergy (see Sections 5.4.1 and 5.4.2) will illustrate top-down market-based forest interventions often perpetuate long-standing patterns of injustices for the same communities that experienced exclusion and violence under colonialism and from settlers' descendants to their lands.

5.3.2 Sustainable Forest Management

Determining whether forest activities are sustainable has a long history in European–US silviculture. Indeed, questions around forest sustainable management predate the principle of sustainable development.[4] In Germany, in the late 18th century, a scientific silvicultural method, the concept of sustainable yield, was developed (Scott 1998). The method was designed to enable foresters to calculate the maximum yield from a forest without resulting in long-term value loss to any given concession. Any extraction was to be offset by rotational reforestation calculated to replenish the forest resource stock within a species-specific timespan. The German scientific method prioritised the extracted timber's market value. Other ecosystem functions such as hydrological, soil composition, and biodiversity habitat were not included in the value calculation. The German scientific method spread far and wide, taking root in forest management administrations in countries around the world. Foresters scattered around Europe's empires and colonies trialled the German scientific method with little understanding of local forest biome diversity or indigenous peoples' and communities' knowledge (Bryant 1997; Guha 1983; Sivaramakrishnan 1995).

The techniques employed by colonial foresters laid the foundations for early principles of environmentalism, such as conservation and sustainable resource management (Barton 2001). Since the 1990s sustainable forest certification schemes, mostly developed by actors in the Global North (international organisations, business, and nongovernmental organisations) have aimed to provide principles, criteria, and systems to guarantee sustainability (Gulbrandsen 2010). The majority of forest commodity trade, either directly or indirectly, as processed products, have flowed from the Global South to the Global North, especially since the 1950s (Hyde 2012). Voluntary certification schemes promised premium market prices to suppliers, mainly in European markets (WWF 2021). Yet, sustainable forest certification schemes, especially the FSC, proved too expensive and incompatible with small- and medium-sized enterprises, as well as marginalised forest communities and indigenous peoples to benefit from (Lesniewska and McDermott 2014).

Forest certification has been accused of being a neo-colonial 'fetishized commodity', part of a new form of extra-territoriality intervention by the Global North, that perpetuates top-down Western scientific models of sustainable certification, paying scant attention to traditional forest communities and indigenous peoples' knowledge reflected in their own customary legal systems (Vandergeest 2016; Pye 2019). As a push-back to established transnational certification schemes countries in the Global South such as Indonesia, Malaysia, and China have chosen to develop their own certification schemes, each with varying degrees of recognition for forest communities and indigenous peoples' rights (Buckingham and Jepson 2013).

Overall certification has not addressed the legacies of colonialism such as distributive inequity, and procedural and representative injustices. Certification schemes do not challenge the consumer-growth-based economic model. Indeed, the integrity of certification schemes has increasingly been questioned. As market demand for certified forest commodities grew certification bodies choose to alter their criteria, for example including certified plantations and mixed recycling making verification of sustainability more difficult. Arguably extending certification to biomass, or even Bioenergy Carbon Capture and Storage (BECCS), within a CFBE will perpetuate the revisionist environmental management approach that will serve only to provide greenwash for companies including those seeking to offset polluting activities from aviation to cement.

5.3.3 Forest Ecosystems: Beyond 'Othering'

There is a growing recognition that any laws dealing with environmental issues, including all natural resources, need to address the fundamental problem that they operate within a system that is at the core of the problem itself (M'Gonigle and Takeda 2013). Prevailing legal systems globally remain lodged in a mechanistic worldview that came to prominence in the Enlightenment – a worldview that assumes non-human nature is subject to human dominance and control through ownership. It is a worldview that supports the reductionist view that measuring and quantifying the discrete elements of a system yields a full understanding of the whole (Capra and Mattei 2015). Within this system, law perpetuates the 'othering of nature' and reproduces the modem 'epistemology of mastery' whereby knowledge is mobilised towards the material control and domination of nature (De Lucia 2017). However, increasingly international and national laws and policies are incorporating alternative paradigms of human relationships with the environment. This is a significant shift from the instrumentalist approach which has dominated environmentalism for several centuries since the colonial period. A key question for the CFBE is whether its laws will contribute to advancing the trend away from an instrumental 'epistemology of mastery' or simply perpetuate it?

The ecological philosopher Thomas Berry (1999) stated that 'ecology is not part of the law; law is an extension of ecology'. Since the 1970s scientific ecological principles, largely developed in the Global North, have increasingly become embedded in law, especially through conservation and biodiversity laws. The reconfiguring of legal ethics is premised on a more intrinsic valuing of nature rather than one that is purely instrumental (Gillespie 2014; Kim and Bosselmann 2015). The 1992 CBD has acted as an international forum to incorporate and develop ecological principles into law. Parties adopted in 2002 the ecosystem approach to guide all work programmes, including on forests, which focused on the need to balance complementary ecosystem attributes of function, structure, and composition in resource management to ensure ecological integrity is maintained.[5] In 2008, scientific research by academics resulted in two new concepts: the Anthropocene and planetary boundaries. Both concepts, although contested for their universalising, ahistorical narratives, rapidly became keystones for subsequent influential research feeding into law and policy-making relating to ecosystems' ecological integrity (Rockström et al. 2008; Steffen et al. 2008; Kotzé 2017). One significant international development was the creation of a new intergovernmental organisation.

To 'strengthen the science-policy interface for biodiversity and ecosystem services for the conservation and sustainable use of biodiversity, long-term human well-being and sustainable development' the independent Intergovernmental Panel on Biodiversity and Ecosystem Services (IPBES) was established in 2012. The IPBES reports have legitimised numerous other law and policy initiatives to recognise ecological integrity and interdependences between all life forms beyond instrumental values including legal recognition of nature rights by courts,[6] a growth in environmental constitutionalism (Boyd 2011; Collins 2021), a drive to recognise the right to a healthy environment within the UN,[7] the new concept of planetary health (Horton et al. 2014; Mair 2020; Myers and Frumkin 2020), and the campaign to have ecocide recognised as a crime against humanity.[8] Collectively, these developments in law represent a paradigm shift away from 'epistemology of mastery', laying the foundations for 'ecological law'.

Ecological law, according to Sbert (2020), demands that extraction, manufacturing, and distribution be carried out without causing serious harm to humans (workers, neighbours, and users/consumers) and other beings, and without diminishing the ecological integrity of the ecosystems within which they take place. As such ecological law challenges the 'dominant anthropocentric narrative gives primacy to economic growth and technological innovation, reinforced by legal systems built around strong notions of state sovereignty and private property rights' (M'Gonigle and Takeda 2013). There is a danger that ecological law could become anchored within a universalising discourse, one that excludes other worldviews from processes to define problems and determine solutions like existing environmental law. Concerns about scientific expertise, conservation managers, and environmental consultants determining the boundaries within which law and policy is developed to maintain ecological integrity exist, especially amongst advocates for representation and procedural justice for marginalised communities and indigenous peoples. To prevent ecological law becoming a new wave of green neo-colonialism which excludes forest communities and indigenous peoples, it is necessary for there to be a transition to a pluriverse in which 'ecologies of knowledge' thrive and are respected (Escobar 2018; Reiter 2018). The following section explains and discusses the importance of transitioning to a pluriverse for future circular forest governance and justice.

5.3.4 Returning to a Pluriverse

Transition discourses calling for new relational ways of being in the world are emerging from a multiplicity of sites including ecological legal jurisprudence, decolonial, race, and feminist scholarship as well as from civil society activists (Fanon 1970; Merchant 1980; Shiva 2005; Stone 2010; Swimme 2019). Escobar (2011) sees 'a transition to an altogether different world' as being a hallmark of these discourses. Reiter (2018) argues that such discourses challenge the globally dominant modern linear epistemology, which has its origins within 18th century European philosophy, that promotes 'one-dimensional solutions to diverse problems'. One influential strand of transition discourse has come from indigenous peoples, especially from several settler colonised countries in Latin America, a region of the world with extensive bio-diverse-rich tropical forests including the Amazon (Ndlovu-Gatsheni 2020; Rodriguez 2021).

Tropical forests in Latin America have since being colonised in the 17th century been plundered not only for timber but increasingly in the late 20th and 21st centuries for land clearance to grow agro-industrial commodities mainly to meet demand from export markets in North America and Europe. Indigenous peoples in the region have throughout this time experienced displacement and violence. Data collected by civil society has for several years documented that Latin American countries are the highest ranked for death and violence towards indigenous peoples, especially amongst communities defending their territorial lands and forests from infrastructure developments and conversion for agro-industrial commodities (Global Witness 2021).

An important means to challenge laws is to identify the underlying epistemological norms informing them. Although indigenous peoples in Latin America have for centuries resisted instrumental legal norms used to legitimise appropriation of territorial lands and resources, progress to articulate alternative epistemologies drawing on traditional knowledge systems has been made in the 21st century. In 2008, both Ecuadorian and Bolivian constitutions introduced a novel notion of development centred on the concept of sumak kawsay (in Quechua), suma qamaña (in Aymara), or buen vivir (in Spanish), or 'living well'. The buen vivir upholds a different philosophy of life into the vision of society, one that subordinates economic objectives to ecological criteria, human dignity, and social justice. In 2008, Ecuador made history when it became the first country in the world to grant nature legally-enforceable constitutional rights to 'exist, flourish and evolve'. The constitutional reforms have already provided legal opportunities to uphold alternative epistemological norms in which forest ecological integrity is prioritised over conversion and extraction. For example, in December 2021, seven justices of the Ecuadorian Constitutional Court ruled that mining activities pursued by a state mining company and its Canadian partner threatened a protected region of the Ecuadorian rainforest and would violate the rights of nature under Article 71 of the country's 2008 Constitution.[9]

The incorporation of alternative epistemological framings in the Latin American constitutions represents, in Escobar's (2011) view, a 'biocentric turn', away from the anthropocentric, instrumental modernity that underpins linear economic laws. Escobar argues that this biocentric turn is indicative of a civilisational transformation imagined by the transitional discourses, one that moves the world away from the 'epistemology of mastery'. The constitutional changes in Latin America have made possible a return to a pluriverse, a world in which there are diverse worldviews co-existing but which are underpinned by ecological legal principles – ecocentrism, ecological primacy, and ecological justice (Collins 2021). This is a world that existed before the modern, instrumentalist linear economy, although how it manifests now will not be as it was.

The pluriverse is being woven into the polycentric global legal order. The 2007 UN Declaration on Rights of Indigenous Peoples was also a catalyst for initiatives around the world that are promoting recognition and procedural justice to influence decision-making processes on law and policy-making. A significant advance for justice in Latin America is the 2018 Escazú Agreement, which guarantees the right to access environmental information and participate in environmental decision-making, promoting access to information and access to justice related to environmental matters while recognising the right to a healthy environment. The Agreement also, importantly for indigenous peoples, requires States to prevent and investigate attacks against those who protect and defend environmental rights.[10]

Global cognitive justice will not be possible unless there is a return to a pluriverse, de Sousa Santos (2014) argues 'it is imperative to recover and valorize the epistemological diversity of the world ... to build a new kind of bottom-up cosmopolitanism in which conviviality, solidarity and life triumph'. Forest ecosystems have been, and remain, at the forefront for indigenous peoples' reclaiming epistemological space to return the world to a pluriverse. Those involved in developing laws and policies for CFBEs need to support and advance the return of a pluriverse.

5.3.5 Summary

Forest-related law throughout the world is founded upon centuries, if not millennia, of socio-cultural precedents and custom. There are challenges and opportunities within existing forest laws for the CFBE. Building on advances in ecological law and recognition of indigenous peoples' worldviews will be important for a future CBFE if it is to overcome the legacies of colonialism and the modern linear economic model. In the next section, we examine two sectors that fall within the CBFE to show how existing forest-related laws, and recent initiatives to address climate change have informed legal design and policy priorities. We discuss how collectively laws and policies within each example individually undermine moving ahead with a CFBE, especially one that does not perpetuate existing inequities and injustices in the current linear global agro-industrial forestry model.

5.4 Case Studies

A cornerstone concept to the CFBE is cascading (Bezama 2016). The cascading principle promotes narrowing the gap between biomass utilisation and the waste hierarchy. Within the EU cascading is defined as 'the efficient utilisation of resources by using residues and recycled materials for material use to extend total biomass availability within a given system' (European Commission 2019). In some biobased sectors, such as in pulp and paper, cascading use already has been established for decades. From a technical perspective, cascading begins when wood is processed into a product and this product is used at least once more either for material or energy purposes. The main targets of cascading within the CFBE are increased resource efficiency and less demand for virgin materials.

In this section, we have chosen to focus on two nodes within the cascading of forest bio-resources. We begin with forest carbon, which is a recent bioproduct created using legal tools. This will be followed by bioenergy. The case studies will show how individual bioresource sectors have their own market dynamics and drivers that undermine the cascading principle. These markets can also have wider equity and justice impacts throughout the supply chain. Obviously, there are other nodes within the cascading cycle of forest bioresources such as wood products used in construction, that in an extended study warrant attention. However despite a limited focus, our conclusion remains the same that if cascading within a CFBE is to be successful, a comprehensive systems approach will need to be adopted, underpinned by laws and policies across the forest-related and lands use sectors.

5.4.1 Forest Carbon Sequestration

Creating new high-value markets is integral to a CFBE if it is to achieve its goals to maximise the use cycle. One of the essential elements of the CE is that circular flows of materials always maintain the highest possible product value for as long as possible (Campbell 2018). Cascading traditionally has focused on products from the point of harvest before any recycling or remanufacturing processes within a waste hierarchy framework. Cascading begins with the decision about how to use the fresh biomass, including whether to harvest it, with a view to conserve carbon sequestration capacity and/or biodiversity habitat for example.

Under the 1992 UNFCCC parties are required to reduce greenhouse gas emissions through land use, land use change, and forestry (LULUCF) activities, as well as increase carbon sequestration to mitigate climate change.[11] Using property, contract, and trade law, it was possible for a new commodity to be created that could be produced (grown) and traded internationally to expand the scope of the BE market: sequestered forest carbon. Building on UNFCCC, the 1997 Kyoto Protocol included flexibility mechanisms that could be used for forestry activities, including the option to trade sequestered carbon from afforestation and reforestation projects. The opportunity to trade sequestered forest carbon was extended to developing countries (Annex 2), through Art. 12, known as the Clean Development Mechanism. Prior to the Kyoto Protocol, no sequestration forest carbon product nor market upon which it could be traded existed anywhere in the world.

At the 2008 UNFCCC Bali Conference of the Parties (COP), the scope for forest carbon trading was widened to include emissions reductions activities that resulted in avoided deforestation and degradation (REDD), not just afforestation and reforestation as it was under the Kyoto Protocol. It was argued by REDD advocates that placing a monetary value on a forest's carbon sequestration capacity would mean the forest would be more valuable standing. The cost-benefit analysis subsequently also took account of co-benefits from undertaking REDD such as biodiversity gains and development opportunities for forest-dependent peoples (Birrell et al. 2012; Pistorius 2012). These purported additional gains were recognised by adding a '+' to the acronym: REDD+. REDD+ forest carbon sequestration policies were, it would appear, an example of a win-win-win for all.

REDD+ was rapidly beset by problems. For REDD+ policy advocates, these were largely technical issues such as how to accurately measure carbon, a necessary requirement if units were to be traded to offset fossil fuel emissions from other sectors (Gifford 2020). Concerns quickly emerged over REDD+ emissions reductions' permanence, as well as a phenomenon referred to as 'leakage', where avoided deforestation in one place could still result in forest loss elsewhere in a country or internationally driven by increasing market demand for wood and/or land by the agro-industrial sectors (Korhonen-Kurki et al. 2013; Streck 2021). Given the global nature of climate change, forest activities generating emissions anywhere would add to the problem everywhere, which undermines the rationale of paying for emissions reductions under a place-based REDD+ system. REDD+ as a market-based mechanism was also not easy to establish, especially in tropical forest countries. Long-standing forest governance issues, including extensive illegal logging and trade, corruption, and money laundering, problematised the operationalisation of REDD+ as a market-based mechanism to valorise standing forests (Dehm 2021). Perhaps the greatest obstacle REDD+ faced, however, was ongoing contested land rights.

After first being introduced in 2008 as a climate change mitigation 'low hanging fruit', REDD+'s promissory narrative of co-benefits by supporters, such as the World Bank, has not delivered at scale for forest communities and indigenous peoples, or even its original advocates. The failure to recognise the interconnections between forest management law and policy with other legal domains such as indigenous peoples' rights, and the associated equity and justice issues bound up in historical legacies, was symptomatic of a techno-scientific model approach imposed by multiple stakeholders which excluded many forest peoples (Gupta 2012; Lesniewska 2019). One of the long-running issues for REDD+ was the problem of recognition and procedural justice. Indigenous peoples and forest communities were either not included in processes or, where they were, they were found to be technocratic processes, failing to keep with principles of the concept of free prior informed consent as set out in the newly adopted UN Declaration on the Rights of Indigenous Peoples.[12] This is not out of line with a CFBE model where the focus remains on the value of the forest product within a cascading system, one that does not prioritise the external socio-ecological and cultural values and rights for forest peoples and non-human species.

5.4.2 Bioenergy

Bioenergy has a leading role in CFBE narratives in which biomaterials are used sequentially throughout an ever-cascading value chain. However, demand for biomass to meet large-scale bioenergy demand can distort a cascading system because materials are combusted to generate energy rather than manufactured, reused, and recycled to maximise value across the life cycle of material flows (Kardung et al. 2021). Not only could the levels of demand for biomass undermine circular cascading principles but it could also result in land grabs. The appropriation of land for industrial agricultural scale production, including biomass, has led, and continues today, to the displacement and/or murder of indigenous peoples and land-based communities (Le Billon and Lujala 2020; Ghosh 2021) As such it is important to interrogate the validity of claims that bioenergy from forest-based feedstocks can play a central role in a CFBE. In this section, we focus on how the EU has sought to address the law and policy tensions over bioenergy, and explore new negative emission technology (NET), BECCS to assess whether it will pose a new threat to establishing a sustainable CBFE.

The demand for biomass in the EU is driven by climate and energy laws. Transnational investment, supported by domestic policy and laws in many countries, especially developed countries, laid the foundations for the increase in modern biofuel production. The Kyoto Protocol ushered in a transformation in world biofuel production that nearly trebled between 2000 and 2014. Approximately 30 percent of the increase came from what are referred to as 'modern biofuels', large-scale agro-industrial biofuel production, used for transport, electricity generation, and urban heating. Biofuel production is predicted to triple once again between 2015 and 2035 (d'Ortigue et al. 2015).

In the EU, the Renewable Energy Directive (RED) set targets for Member States to replace fossil fuels with bioenergy. However, RED Art. 17 excluded biomass from the sustainability and carbon accounting criteria set for bioliquids used for transportation.[13] Many EU countries switched to using biomass feedstock, such as forest residues from harvesting and production processes, as an alternative to fossil fuels for electricity power stations. Repurposing residues to valorise the forest resource loop is framed as a positive contribution to creating a sustainable CFBE, one that can help to mitigate climate change and create new green business models (Zabaniotou 2018). RED's incentivisation of wood-burning for energy means that about 55 percent of the EU wood harvest are burnt for energy, up from slightly more than 40 percent in 2005. During this time, the capacity of forests to absorb carbon declined by 28 percent (FERN 2022). To meet demand, the EU needs to import biomass primarily from the United States and Russia (Brack 2017). The Ukraine war has highlighted EU dependency on Russian imports for biomass, as well as timber (Ro 2022).

Civil society organisations concerned about the sourcing of biomass from primary forests, both within EU member states and from exporter countries like the United States and Russia, rather than residues, welcomed a revision to EU biomass sustainability criteria (Taylor and Romano 2022). Both the RED and the Regulation on LULUCF include a new definition for primary woody biomass.[14] Apart from certain exemptions, woody biomass would no longer be considered as renewable energy and no longer be eligible for incentives meant to promote renewables. Secondary woody biomass, such as sawdust, black liquor, and post-consumer wood waste, would still count as renewable, arguably to incentivise cascading from up the value chain.[15]

The amendment on sustainability criteria for biomass materials by the EU Commission is an important step to close the loopholes that enabled high-value woody materials to be burnt for energy. However, it comes at a time there is a push to adopt NET to achieve rapid decarbonisation. The bioequivalent of NET is BECCS. BECCS promises to combine biomass energy generation with strategies to sequester carbon through both large-scale afforestation and reforestation as well as sequestration technology. The primary technology upon which large-scale negative emissions from BECCS would be based is industrial-scale thermochemical gasification of biomass to produce a gaseous fuel. This gaseous fuel is then used either to power production or – at lower sequestration rates – for use as a synthesis gas for biofuel production, allowing for a stream of carbon dioxide to be extracted, compressed, and sequestered in a geological reservoir (Dooley and Kartha 2018). BECCS is using technology that some argue is more efficient than a natural forest as it is not subject to sink saturation limits because the carbon is sequestered in geological reservoirs.

BECCS will primarily be reliant on large-scale biomass feedstock supplies, which are ultimately limited by natural capacity. BECCS' reliance on afforestation and reforestation has numerous problems in terms of monitoring and reporting actual greenhouse gas emissions. Also, BECCS requires dedicated land use to offset negative emissions options, which places pressure on food supplies by reducing the availability of land for food production (Smith et al. 2014). BECCS, a form of monocultural plantation, will replace existing biodiverse-rich forests, or take spaces where dedicated biodiverse-rich forests could be planted. Although under the UNFCCC definition of forests BECCS could be counted as increasing forest coverage globally and included as a forest carbon sequestration mitigation activity within a Nationally Determined Contribution under the Paris Agreement, it will do so at the expense of biodiversity rich habitat and ecological integrity.

Linking carbon markets with BECCS is another concern. Planting trees to offset polluting activities will have impacts on land use options for countries. For example, Oxfam (2021) found that the 'net-zero' climate promises of four of the world's largest oil and gas corporations – BP, Eni, Shell, and Total Energies – could require them to forest an area of land equivalent to more than twice the size of the United Kingdom to achieve net zero by 2050 combined. BECCS is already raising concerns that it will drive land grabs, especially from forest communities and indigenous peoples, like those that occurred after the Kyoto Protocol when developed countries, especially in the EU, adopted renewable energy quotas, including bioenergy. Forest carbon offsetting and BECCS will drive further eco-colonialisation and appropriation of forest peoples' lands and other species habitats (Dooley et al. 2018; Vigil 2018).

Increased demand for bioenergy materials, including those to support BECCS, will not be met through a circular cascade model when the market demand is greater than available supply within a cascade system. Given the potential negative social and environmental impacts from modern large-scale bioenergy, as well as the new NET policy BECCS, that are reliant on forest materials it is necessary to ask how such a resource use model meets the goals for a CBFE.

5.4.3 Summary

Cascading is a core concept for the CBFE. As this section has demonstrated currently key sectors within a cascading model for the CBFE do not operate in an integrated and aligned manner, rather they are fragmented and driven by independent dynamic forces, stimulated by laws and policies, acting on the value chain. Each of the case studies covered is increasingly being shaped by climate change laws primarily to reduce greenhouse gas emissions, not any goal to deliver an integrated sustainable, just, and inclusive CBFE.

5.5 Conclusion

The CFBE is presented, as are other CE sectors, as a promissory opportunity in which all stakeholders could benefit. What the CFBE appears to be doing though is replicating an economic model in which the value of forest resources is extracted and distributed amongst a small number of stakeholders. This is a silvicultural model that is underpinned by an epistemology of the mastery of nature in which forest resources only have commercial instrumental value. It is an economic model that has its roots in the colonial era, a period where the natural resources commercialisation was embedded within legal systems, especially the domains of investment, contract, and property law. Under such an economic system, those stakeholders who are most dependent, and who have traditional knowledge of forest ecosystems, are the ones who benefit least and experience the greatest burden from environmental, economic, and social impacts.

This chapter has demonstrated how within two areas of the CBFE model, based on a cascading hierarchical relational approach, current laws and policies are failing to engender a systemic closed-loop circular model. Each of the case study areas – forest carbon and bioenergy – appear to operate in separate markets and have differing dynamics driving commercial priorities. The CBFE, mainly driven by net zero greenhouse gas mitigation priorities set out in the UNFCCC's 2015 Paris Agreement, appears to be repeating mistakes that have so often led to injustices for forest-based communities and indigenous peoples. Alternative approaches are emerging, however, such as ecological laws and epistemological paradigms that recognise a diverse pluriverse will add to global resilience, replacing the mono-epistemological legacy of colonialism and modernism.

Notes

1 See Decision11/CP.7 on Land-use, land-use change, and forestry, UNFCCC/SBSTA (Marrakech Accord).
2 See CBD, Expanded Programme of Work on Forest Biological Diversity 2002 decision VI/22, para 10, Annex.
3 See UNDP's Paris Agreement LULUCF and NDC Tool (PLANT), which analyses countries' opportunities to enhance the contribution of the forest sector to nationally determined contributions mitigation targets. Available at: https://data.undp.org/content/plant-paris-agreement-lulucf-assessment-ndc-tool/.
4 Sustainable development was first formally recognised internationally in 1992 – See Principle 2 Rio Declaration on Environment and Development

1992, Report of the United Nations Conference on Environment and Development, Rio de Janeiro, 3–14 June 1992.

5 The ecosystem approach is a strategy for the integrated management of land, water, and living resources that promotes conservation and sustainable use in an equitable way guided by 12 complementary and interlinked principles. All work under the CBD is required to adhere to the ecosystem approach including forests. See also COP 5 decision V/6.

6 For example: Te Awa Tupua Act (Whanganui River Claims Settlement), No. 7, 2017 (New Zealand); Centro de Estudios para la Justicia Social 'Tierra Digna' v. President of the Republic, NoT-5.016.242, Corte Constitucional, Sala Sexta de Revision [Constitutional Court, Sixth Chamber], 10 Nov. 2016, (Colombia); Caso No. 1149-19-Jp/20 El Pleno de la Corte Constitucional del Ecuador, en Ejercicio de Sus Atribuciones Constitucionales y Legales, expide la Siguiente, 10 de Noviembre de 2021 (Ecuador).

7 The human right to a clean, healthy and sustainable environment: draft resolution, UNGA Res A/76/L.75 28 July 2022.

8 See End Ecocide International Criminal Court petition: <U>https://www.endecocide.org/en/sign-the-new-international-petition/.</U>

9 Caso No. 1149-19-Jp/20 El Pleno De La Corte Constitucional Del Ecuador, En Ejercicio De Sus Atribuciones Constitucionales Y Legales, Expide La Siguiente (Spanish only). http://esacc.corteconstitucional.gob.ec/storage/api/v1/10_DWL_FL/e2NhcnBldGE6J3RyYW1pdGUnLCB-1dWlkOic2MmE3MmIxNy1hMzE4LTQyZmMtYjJkOS1mYzYzNWE5Z-TAwNGYucGRmJ30=.

10 Regional Agreement on Access to Information, Public Participation and Justice in Environmental Matters in Latin America and the Caribbean, (Escazú Agreement), 4 March 2018. www.cepal.org/en/escazuagreement.

11 Under UNFCCC (1992) Art. 4(1)(d) identifies a commitment to promote sustainable management, and promote and cooperate in the conservation and enhancement, as appropriate, of sinks and reservoirs of all greenhouse gases not controlled by the Montreal Protocol, including biomass, forests, and oceans as well as other terrestrial, coastal, and marine ecosystems. Art. 4(1)(a) identifies further commitment to develop, periodically update, publish and make available to the COP, in accordance with Art. 12, national inventories of anthropogenic emissions by sources and removals by sinks of all greenhouse gases not controlled by the Montreal Protocol, using comparable methodologies to be agreed upon by the COP.

12 See Art. 19 of 61/295. United Nations Declaration on the Rights of Indigenous Peoples, 13 September 2007.

13 Renewable Energy Directive 2009/28/EC on the promotion of the use of energy from renewable sources.

14 Amending Renewable Energy Directive (EU) 2018/2001 24 June 2022; Proposal for a Regulation of the European Parliament and of the Council amending Regulations (EU) 2018/841 as regards the scope, simplifying the compliance rules, setting out the targets of the Member States for 2030 and committing to the collective achievement of climate neutrality by 2035 in the land use, forestry, and agriculture sector, and (EU) 2018/1999 as regards improvement in monitoring, reporting, tracking of progress and review, 28 June 2022.

15 Ibid.

References

Arts, B., Appelstrand, M., Kleinschmit, D., Pülz, H., Visseren-Hamakers, I., Atyi, R.E., Enters, T., McGinley, K. and Yasmi, Y. 2010. In: *Embracing Complexity: Meeting the Challenges of International Forest Governance. A Global Assessment Report.* Forest and Nature Conservation Policy.

Barañano, L., Garbisu, N., Alkorta, I., Araujo, A. and Garbisu, C. 2021. Contextualization of the bioeconomy concept through its links with related concepts and the challenges facing humanity. *Sustainability*, 13(14), p.7746. https://doi.org/10.3390/su13147746.

Barton, G. 2001. Empire forestry and the origins of environmentalism. *Journal of Historical Geography*, 27(4), pp.529–552. https://doi.org/10.1006/jhge.2001.0353.

Bastos Lima, M.G. and Palme, U. 2021. The bioeconomy–biodiversity nexus: enhancing or undermining nature's contributions to people? *Conservation*, 2(1), pp.7–25. https://doi.org/10.3390/conservation2010002.

Berry, T. 1999. *The Great Work: Our Way into the Future.* New York: Three Rivers Press.

Bezama, A. 2016. Let us discuss how cascading can help implement the circular economy and the bio-economy strategies. *Waste Management and Research*, 34(7), pp.593–594. https://doi.org/10.1177/0734242X16657973.

Birrell, K., Godden, L. and Tehan, M. 2012. Climate change and REDD+: property as a prism for conceiving indigenous peoples' engagement. *Journal of Human Rights and the Environment*, 3(2), pp.196–216. https://doi.org/10.4337/jhre.2012.03.02.

Bisang, R. and Trigo, E. 2018. *Bioeconomía Argentina. Modelos de negocios para una nueva matriz productive.* www.magyp.gob.ar/sitio/areas/bioeconomia/_archivos//Modelo_de_negocios.pdf.

Boyd, D.R. 2011. *The Environmental Rights Revolution: A Global Study of Constitutions, Human Rights, and the Environment.* UBC Press.

Brack, D. 2017. *The Impacts of the Demand for Woody Biomass for Power and Heat on Climate and Forests.* Chatham House, the Royal Institute of International Affairs.

Brandão, A.S., Goncalves, A. and Santos, J.M. 2021. Circular bioeconomy strategies: from scientific research to commercially viable products. *Journal of Cleaner Production*, 295, p.126407. https://doi.org/10.1016/j.jclepro.2021.126407.

Bryant, R.L. 1997. *The Political Ecology of Forestry in Burma: 1824–1994.* University of Hawaii Press.

Buckingham, K. and Jepson, P. 2013. Forest certification with Chinese characteristics: state engagement with non-state market-driven governance. *Eurasian Geography and Economics*, 54(3), pp.280–299. https://doi.org/10.1080/15387216.2013.849850.

Campbell, A. 2018. Mass timber in the circular economy: paradigm in practice? *Proceedings of the Institution of Civil Engineers - Engineering Sustainability*, 172(3), pp.141–152. https://doi.org/10.1680/jensu.17.00069.

Capra, F. and Mattei, U. 2015. *The Ecology of Law: Toward a Legal System in Tune with Nature and Community.* San Francisco: Berrett Koehler.

Carus, M. and Dammer, L. 2018. The circular bioeconomy – concepts, opportunities, and limitations. *Industrial Biotechnology,* 14(2), pp.83–91. https://doi.org/10.1089/ind.2018.29121.mca.

CEFO (Confederation of European Forest Owners). 2017. *Private Forest Owners Call for An Ambitious Update of the EU Bioeconomy Strategy;* Confederation of European Forest Owners: Brussels, Belgium.

Chazdon, R.L., Brancalion, P.H., Laestadius, L., Bennett-Curry, A., Buckingham, K., Kumar, C., Moll-Rocek, J., Vieira, I.C.G. and Wilson, S.J. 2016. When is a forest a forest? Forest concepts and definitions in the era of forest and landscape restoration. *Ambio,* 45(5), pp.538–550. https://doi.org/10.1007/s13280-016-0772-y.

CIFOR (Centre for International Forestry Research). 2021. *The Circular Bioeconomy: Knowledge Guide.* www.cifor.org/wp-content/uploads/2021/03/Flyer%20-%20Knowledge%20Guide_Circular%20Bioeconomy-v4.pdf.

Collins, L. 2021. *The Ecological Constitution: Reframing Environmental Law.* Routledge.

Cullen, J.M. 2017. Circular economy: theoretical benchmark or perpetual motion machine? *Journal of Industrial Ecology,* 21(3), pp.483–486. https://doi.org/10.1111/jiec.12599.

d'Ortigue, O. L., Whiteman, A. and Elsayed, S. 2015. *Renewable Energy Capacity Statistics* 2015. IRENA. www.irena.org/-/media/Files/IRENA/Agency/Publication/2015/IRENA_RE_Capacity_Statistics_2015.pdf.

D'Adamo, I., Gastaldi, M., Morone, P., Rosa, P., Sassanelli, C., Settembre-Blundo, D. and Shen, Y. 2022. Bioeconomy of sustainability: drivers, opportunities and policy implications. *Sustainability,* 14(1), p.200. https://doi.org/10.3390/su14010200.

D'Amato, D., Droste, N., Winkler, K.J. and Toppinen. 2019. Thinking green, circular or bio: eliciting researchers' perspectives on a sustainable economy with Q method. *Journal of Cleaner Production,* 230, pp.460–476. https://doi.org/10.1016/j.jclepro.2019.05.099.

De Lucia, V. 2017. Critical environmental law and the double register of the Anthropocene: a biopolitical reading. In: Kotzé, L. (Ed.). *Environmental Law and Governance for the Anthropocene.* Hart Publishing. https://doi.org/10.5040/9781509906574.ch-005.

de Sousa Santos, B. 2014. *Epistemologies of the South. Justice Against Epistemicide.* Routledge. https://doi.org/10.4324/9781315634876.

Deciancio, M., Siegel, K. M., Kefeli, D., de Queiroz Stein, G. and Dietz, T. 2022. Bioeconomy governance and (sustainable) development. In: Deciancio, M., Nemiña, P. and Tussie, D. (Eds.). *Handbook on the Politics of International Development,* pp. 329–345. Edward Elgar Publishing.

Dehm, J. 2021. *Reconsidering REDD+: Authority, Power and Law in the Green Economy.* Cambridge University Press.

Dooley, K. and Kartha, S. 2018. Land-based negative emissions: risks for climate mitigation and impacts on sustainable development. *International*

Environmental Agreements: Politics, Law and Economics, 18(1), pp.79–98. https://doi.org/10.1007/s10784-017-9382-9.

Dooley, K., Christoff, P. and Nicholas, K. A. 2018. Co-producing climate policy and negative emissions: trade-offs for sustainable land-use. *Global Sustainability*, 1, E3. https://doi.org/10.1017/sus.2018.6.

Ellen MacArthur Foundation. 2022. *The Circular Economy* https://archive. ellenmacarthurfoundation.org/explore/the-circular-economy-in-detail.

Escobar, A. 2011. Sustainability: design for the pluriverse. *Development*, 54, pp.137–140. https://doi.org/10.1057/dev.2011.28.

Escobar, A. 2018. Transition discourses and the politics of relationality: towards designs for the pluriverse. In: Reiter, B. (Ed.), *Constructing the Pluriverse: The Geopolitics of Knowledge*, pp.63–89. Duke University Press. https://doi.org/10.1515/9781478002017-005.

European Commission. 2018. *A Sustainable Bioeconomy for Europe: Strengthening the Connection between Economy, Society and the Environment - updated Bioeconomy Strategy*. https://data.europa.eu/doi/10.2777/792130.

European Commission. 2019. *Guidance on Cascading Use of Biomass with Selected Good Practice Example on Woody Biomass*. https://op.europa.eu/en/ publication-detail/-/publication/9b823034-ebad-11e8-b690-01aa75ed71a1.

Fairhead, J., Leach, M. and Scoones, I. 2012. Green grabbing: a new appropriation of nature? *Journal of Peasant Studies*, 39(2), pp.237–261. https://doi. org/10.1080/03066150.2012.671770.

Fanon, F. 1970. *Black Skin, White Masks*. London: Paladin.

FERN. 2022. RED and LULUCF: EU Council prioritises the short-term interests of wood-based industries over the future of forests. www.fern.org/ publications-insight/red-and-lulucf-eu-council-prioritises-the-short-term-interests-of-wood-based-industries-over-the-future-of-forests-2543/.

Foster, J.B. and Clark, B. 2020. *The Robbery of Nature: Capitalism and the Ecological Rift*. Monthly Review Press.

Galaz, V., Biermann, F., Folke, C., Nilsson, M. and Olsson, P. 2012. Global environmental governance and planetary boundaries: an introduction. *Ecological Economics*, 81, pp.1–3. https://doi.org/10.1016/j. ecolecon.2012.02.023.

Garzuglia, M. 2018, *1948–2018: Seventy Years of FAO's Global Forest Resources Assessment - Historical Overview and Future Prospects*, FAO. www.fao.org/3/I8227EN/i8227en.pdf.

Gawel, E., Pannicke, N. and Hagemann, N. 2019. A path transition towards a bioeconomy – the crucial role of sustainability. *Sustainability*, 11(11), p.3005. https://doi.org/10.3390/su11113005.

Georgescu-Roegen, N. 1975. Energy and economic myths. *Southern Economic Journal*, 41(3), pp.347–381. https://doi.org/10.2307/1056148.

Ghosh, A. 2021. *The Nutmeg's Curse: Parables for a Planet in Crisis*. University of Chicago Press.

Giampietro, M. 2019. On the circular bioeconomy and decoupling: implications for sustainable growth. *Ecological Economics*, 162, pp.143–156. https:// doi.org/10.1016/j.ecolecon.2019.05.001.

Giessen, L. 2013. Reviewing the main characteristics of the international forest regime complex and partial explanations for its fragmentation. *International Forestry Review*, 15(1), pp.60–70. https://doi.org/10.1505/146554813805927192.

Gifford, L. 2020. "You can't value what you can't measure": a critical look at forest carbon accounting. *Climatic Change*, 161, pp.291–306. https://doi.org/10.1007/s10584-020-02653-1.

Gillespie, A. 2014. *International Environmental Law, Policy, and Ethics.* Oxford University Press.

Global Forest Watch. 2020. *Forest Monitoring Designed for Action.* www.globalforestwatch.org.

Global Witness. 2021. Last Line of Defence: The Industries Causing the Climate Crisis against Land and Environmental Defenders. www.globalwitness.org/en/campaigns/environmental-activists/last-line-defence/.

Grassi, G., Fiorese, G., Pilli, R., Jonsson, K., Blujdea, V., Korosuo, A. and Vizzarri, M. 2021. *Brief on the Role of the Forest-based Bioeconomy in Mitigating Climate Change through Carbon Storage and Material Substitution.* European Commission. https://publications.jrc.ec.europa.eu/repository/handle/JRC124374.

Guha, R. 1983. Forestry in British and post-British India: a historical analysis. *Economic and Political Weekly*, pp.1882–1896.

Gulbrandsen, L.H. 2010. *Transnational Environmental Governance: The Emergence and Effects of the Certification of Forest and Fisheries.* Edward Elgar Publishing.

Gupta, J. 2012. Glocal forest and REDD+ governance: win–win or lose–lose?. *Current Opinion in Environmental Sustainability*, 4(6), 620–627. https://doi.org/10.1016/j.cosust.2012.09.014.

Hahn, T., McDermott, C., Ituarte-Lima, C., Schultz, M., Green, T. and Tuvendal, M. 2015. Purposes and degrees of commodification: economic instruments for biodiversity and ecosystem services need not rely on markets or monetary valuation. *Ecosystem Services*, 16, pp.74–82. https://doi.org/10.1016/j.ecoser.2015.10.012.

Horton, R., Beaglehole, R., Bonita, R., Raeburn, J., McKee, M. and Wall, S. 2014. From public to planetary health: a manifesto. *Lancet*, 383(9920), p.847. https://doi.org/10.1016/S0140-6736(14)60409-8.

Hyde, W.F. 2012. *The Global Economics of Forestry.* Routledge.

International Advisory Council on Global Bioeconomy. 2020. *Joint Vision for a Global Sustainable Bioeconomy.* www.iacgb.net/PUBLICATIONS.

IPBES. 2019. *Global Assessment Report on Biodiversity and Ecosystem Services of the Intergovernmental Science-Policy Platform on Biodiversity and Ecosystem Services* [Brondizio, E.S., Settele, J., Díaz, S. and Ngo H.T. (Eds.)]. IPBES Secretariat, Bonn, Germany. https://doi.org/10.5281/zenodo.3831673.

IPCC. 2019. Summary for policymakers. In: Shukla, P.R., Skea, J., Calvo Buendia, E. and Masson-Delmotte, V. et al. (Eds.), *Climate Change and Land: An IPCC Special Report on Climate Change, Desertification, Land*

Degradation, Sustainable Land Management, Food Security, and Greenhouse Gas Fluxes in Terrestrial Ecosystems.

Kardung, M., Cingiz, K., Costenoble, O., Delahaye, R., Heijman, W., Lovrić, M. et al. 2021. Development of the circular bioeconomy: drivers and indicators. *Sustainability*, 13(1), p.413. https://doi.org/10.3390/su13010413.

Khan, F. and Ali, Y. 2022. Moving towards a sustainable circular bio-economy in the agriculture sector of a developing country. *Ecological Economics*, 196, p.107402. https://doi.org/10.1016/j.ecolecon.2022.107402.

Kim, R.E. and Bosselmann, K. 2015. Operationalizing sustainable development: ecological integrity as a *grundnorm* of international law. *Review of European, Comparative and International Environmental Law*, 24(2), pp.194–208. https://doi.org/10.1111/reel.12109.

Korhonen-Kurki, K., Brockhaus, M., Duchelle, A. E., Atmadja, S., Thu Thuy, P. and Schofield, L. 2013. Multiple levels and multiple challenges for measurement, reporting and verification of REDD+. *International Journal of the Commons*, 7(2), pp.344–366. https://doi.org/10.18352/ijc.372.

Kotzé, L. (Ed.). 2017. *Environmental Law and Governance for the Anthropocene*. Bloomsbury Publishing.

Le Billon, P. and Lujala, P. 2020. Environmental and land defenders: global patterns and determinants of repression. *Global Environmental Change*, 65, p.102163. https://doi.org/10.1016/j.gloenvcha.2020.102163.

Lesniewska, F. 2016. Forests: learning lessons from our interventions. In: Morgera, E. and Kulovesi, K. (Eds.), *Research Handbook on International Law and Natural Resources*. Edward Elgar Publishing.

Lesniewska, F. 2019. Forests, people and poverty: failing to reform the global development paradigm. In: Cullet, P. and Koonan, S. (Eds.), *Research Handbook on Law, Environment and the Global South*. Edward Elgar Publishing.

Lesniewska, F. and McDermott, C.L. 2014. FLEGT VPAs: Laying a pathway to sustainability via legality lessons from Ghana and Indonesia. *Forest Policy and Economics*, 48, pp.16–23. https://doi.org/10.1016/j.forpol.2014.01.005.

Liobikiene, G., Balezentis, T., Streimikiene, D., and Chen, X. 2019. Evaluation of bioeconomy in the context of strong sustainability. *Sustainable Development*, 27(5), pp.955–964. https://doi.org/10.1002/sd.1984.

Lund, H.G. 2002. When is a forest not a forest? *Journal of Forestry*, 100(8), pp.21–28. https://doi.org/10.1093/jof/100.8.21.

M'Gonigle, M. and Takeda, L. 2013. The liberal limits of environmental law: a green legal critique. *Pace Environmental Law Review*, 30 (3), pp.1005–1115.

Mair, S. 2020. Neoliberal economics, planetary health, and the COVID-19 pandemic: a Marxist ecofeminist analysis. *Lancet*, 4(12), pp.E588–E596. https://doi.org/10.1016/S2542-5196(20)30252-7.

Merchant, C. 1990. *The Death of Nature: Women, Ecology, and the Scientific Revolution*. Harper Collins.

Millennium Ecosystem Assessment, 2005. *Ecosystems and Human Well-being: Synthesis*. Island Press.

Mittra, J. and Zoukas, G. 2020. Unpacking the concept of bioeconomy: problems of definition, measurement, and value. *Science and Technology Studies*, 33(1), pp.2–21. https://doi.org/10.23987/sts.69662.

Moore, C. 2015. *Natural Resources Law*. Thomson Reuters (Professional) Australia Limited.

Myers, S. and Frumkin, H. 2020. *Planetary Health. Protecting Nature to Protect Ourselves*. Island Press.

Ndlovu-Gatsheni, S.J. 2020. Global economy of knowledge in transformative global studies: decoloniality, ecologies of knowledges, and pluriversity. In: Hosseini, H., Goodman, J., Motta, S. and Gills, B.K. *The Routledge Handbook of Transformative Global Studies*, pp. 69–83. Routledge. https://doi.org/10.4324/9780429470325.

OECD. 2019. *Tackling Vulnerability in the Informal Economy*. www.oecd.org/dev/tackling-vulnerability-in-the-informal-economy-939b7bcd-en.htm.

Oxfam. 2021. *Tightening the Net*. www.oxfam.org/en/research/tightening-net-implications-net-zero-climate-targets-land-and-food-equity.

Parfitt, R. 2019. *The Process of International Legal Reproduction: Inequality, Historiography, Resistance*. Cambridge University Press. https://doi.org/10.1017/9781108655118.

Pistorius, T. 2012. From RED to REDD+: the evolution of a forest-based mitigation approach for developing countries. *Current Opinion in Environmental Sustainability*, 4(6), pp.638–645. https://doi.org/10.1016/j.cosust.2012.07.002.

Pye, O. 2019. Commodifying sustainability: development, nature and politics in the palm oil industry. *World Development*, 121, pp.218–228. https://doi.org/10.1016/j.worlddev.2018.02.014.

Reiter, B. (Ed.). 2018. *Constructing the Pluriverse: The Geopolitics of Knowledge*. Duke University Press.

Rights and Resources Initiative. 2015. *Who Owns the World's Land? A Global Baseline of Formally recognized Indigenous and Community Land Rights*. www.rightsandresources.org/wpcontent/uploads/GlobalBaseline_web.pdf.

Ro. C. 2022. Environment NGOs urge an end to Russian wood imports amidst war with Ukraine. *Forbes*. www.forbes.com/sites/christinero/2022/03/03/environment-ngos-urge-an-end-to-russian-wood-imports-amidst-war-with-ukraine/.

Rockström, J., Steffen, W., Noone, K., Folke, C., Sörlin, S., Broman, D., Svedin, U., Persson, Å., Nykvist, B. and Karlberg, L. 2008, *Steering Away from Catastrophic Thresholds: Planetary Boundaries for Human Survival*. Background paper for the Tällberg Pre-Forum Workshop, 24–26th of June 2008.

Rodriguez, I. 2021. The Latin American decolonial environmental justice approach. In: Coolssaet. B. (Ed.). *Environmental Justice. Key issues*. Earthscan Routledge.

Sasaki, N. and Putz, F.E. 2009. Critical need for new definitions of "forest" and "forest degradation" in global climate change agreements. *Conservation Letters*, 2(5), pp.226–232. https://doi.org/10.1111/j.1755-263X.2009.00067.x.

Sbert, C. 2020. *The Lens of Ecological Law: A Look at Mining.* Cheltenham: Edward Elgar.

Scott, J.C. 1998. *Seeing like a State: How Certain Schemes to Improve the Human Condition have Failed.* Yale University Press.

Shiva, V. 2005. *Earth Democracy: Justice, Sustainability and Peace.* Zed Books.

Sivaramakrishnan, K. 1995. Colonialism and forestry in India: imagining the past in present politics. *Comparative Studies in Society and History,* 37(1), pp.3–40.

Smith, P., Clark, H., Dong, H., Elsiddig, E.A., Haberl, H., Harper, R., House, J., Jafari, M. et al. 2014. Chapter 11- Agriculture, forestry and other land use (AFOLU). In: *Climate Change 2014: Mitigation of Climate Change. IPCC Working Group III Contribution to AR5.* Cambridge University Press.

Stark, S., Biber-Freudenberger, L., Dietz, T., Escobar, N., Förster, J. J., Henderson and Börner, J. 2022. Sustainability implications of transformation pathways for the bioeconomy. *Sustainable Production and Consumption,* 29, pp.215–227. https://doi.org/10.1016/j.spc.2021.10.011.

Steffen, W., Crutzen, P., McNeill, J. and Hibbard, K.A. 2008. Stages of the Anthropocene: assessing the human impact on the Earth System. In: *AGU Fall Meeting Abstracts,* GC22B-01.

Stegmann, P., Londo, M. and Junginger, M. 2020. The circular bioeconomy: its elements and role in European bioeconomy clusters. *Resources, Conservation and Recycling: X,* 6, p.100029. https://doi.org/10.1016/j.rcrx.2019.100029.

Stone, D. 2010. *Histories of the Holocaust.* Oxford University Press.

Streck, C. 2021. REDD+ and leakage: debunking myths and promoting integrated solutions. *Climate Policy,* 21(6), pp.843–852. https://doi.org/10.1080/14693062.2021.1920363.

Swimme, B.T. 2019. *Hidden Heart of the Cosmos: Humanity and the New Story.* Orbis Books.

Tacconi, L., Boscolo, M. and Brack, D. 2003. National and international policies to control illegal forest activities. *Royal Institute of International Affairs.* www.cifor.org/publications/pdf_files/events/Illegal-logging.pdf.

Taylor, K. and Romano, V. 2022. Campaigners hail 'historic breakthrough' on revised EU biomass rules. *Euractiv.* www.euractiv.com/section/energy/news/campaigners-hail-historic-breakthrough-on-revised-eu-biomass-rules/.

Trines, E., Höhne, N., Jung, M., Skutsch, M.M., Petsonk, A., Silva-Chavez, G., Smith, P., Nabuurs, G.J., Verweij, P.A. and Schlamadinger, B. 2006. *Climate Change: Scientific Assessment and Policy Analysis. Integrating Agriculture, Forestry and other Land Use in Future Climate Regimes. Methodological Issues and Policy Options.* Netherlands Environmental Assessment Agency.

United Nations Environment Programme International Resource Panel (UNEP-IRP). 2019. *Global Resources Outlook 2019: Natural Resources for the Future We Want.* https://wedocs.unep.org/handle/20.500.11822/27517.

Van Noordwijk, M. and Minang, P. 2009. If we cannot define it, we cannot save it: forest definitions and REDD. *ASB Policy Brief, 15.*

Vandergeest, P. 2016. Transnational sustainability certification as a new extraterritoriality? In: Antons, C. (Ed.), *Routledge Handbook of Asian Law,* pp. 285–300. New York: Routledge. https://doi.org/10.4324/9781315660547.

Vigil, S. 2018. Green grabbing-induced displacement. In: McLeman, R. and Gemenne, F. (Eds.), *Routledge Handbook of Environmental Displacement and Migration,* pp.370–387. Routledge.

Vivien, F.-D., Nieddu, M., Befort, N., Debref, R. and Giampietro, M. 2019. The hijacking of the bioeconomy. *Ecological Economics,* 159, pp.189–197. https://doi.org/10.1016/j.ecolecon.2019.01.027.

White, A. and Martin, A., 2002. *Who Owns the World's Forests?* Washington: Forest Trends.

Williams, M. 2003. *Deforesting the Earth: From Prehistory to Global Crisis.* University of Chicago Press.

WWF. 2021. EU consumption responsible for 16% of tropical deforestation linked to international trade. https://www.wwf.eu/?2831941/ EU-consumption-responsible-for-16-of-tropical-deforestation-linked-to-international-trade.

Zabaniotou, A. 2018. Redesigning a bioenergy sector in EU in the transition to circular waste-based bioeconomy - a multidisciplinary review. *Journal of Cleaner Production,* 177, pp.197–206. https://doi.org/10.1016/j. jclepro.2017.12.172.

6   Case Study Analysis

In this final chapter before the conclusion, we analyse the two case studies presented in Chapters 4 and 5: circular plastics and the circular forest bioeconomy (CFBE), respectively. In our analysis, we use Kirchherr et al.'s (2017) conceptual framing of the circular economy (CE) around five themes introduced and reviewed in Chapter 1 in addition to drawing on observations and arguments articulated in Chapters 2 and 3. We question whether there are extant serious shortcomings in laws and policies being pursued to advance transitions to CEs. We further explore how bringing justice into the framing of CEs will facilitate explicit engagement with these challenges to enable CE implementations beyond current predominantly 'same-but-circular-business' models.

6.1 Introduction

After analysing more than 100 CE definitions, Kirchherr et al. (2017) identified five key themes framing the CE concept: (1) waste; (2) prevention, reuse, recycling, and recovery of materials and waste; (3) sustainable development; (4) scale; and (5) social equity for the benefit of current and future generations (see Section 1.3). The scope of Kirchherr et al.'s CE is broad. Unlike most CE definitions, it explicitly acknowledges social equity for current and future generations within its conceptual frame. In the analysis of CE sector case studies set out in this chapter, it is evident that, although social equity is a category on its own within Kirchherr et al.'s concept, it is also a crosscutting theme that has relevance for the other four themes. Consider, for example, the theme of 'scale': a globalised techno-industrial CE in which a few oligopolies control material value chains will potentially exacerbate long-standing inequities for current and/or future generations, even

DOI: 10.4324/9780429355141-6

if there are gains in resource efficiencies and waste reduction in the economy.

Observations about each of Kirchherr et al.'s (2017) five CE themes in relation to the two case study sectors previously covered in this book – circular plastics and the CFBE – are set out in the following sections. Both case studies provide experiences and observations we believe indicative of those forthcoming in other sectors committing to increasing circularity and transitioning to CEs. We highlight several similarities across the two sectors in the challenges they are facing to determine pathways to sustainable, just, and inclusive circular futures. There are also distinctive problems that each sector faces, which are also noted, with implications for their transition journey considered.

6.2 Waste

Contested concepts and definitions within law are nothing new. Yet within the CE each definition has implications for how waste within sectors is defined and categorised, with ultimate implications for opportunities to increase circularity. For instance, like the CE, there are no single definitions in law of plastics, plastic wastes, bioeconomy (BE), or a forest. Some plastics' definitions have specific chemical formulae, but the absence of common definitions is not (yet) regarded as problematic. There are, however, some waste definitional and categorisation challenges. Some characteristics and related standards of plastics (e.g., compostable vs. biodegradable) have been identified as problematic. There are opportunities to address these challenges through harmonising standards in the mandated global plastics treaty.

The absence of a single definition can also provide flexibility and open up opportunities for more community and indigenous knowledge-based approaches. This is certainly the case with the CFBE. The case study shows that increased incorporation of the United Nations Framework Convention on Climate Change (UNFCCC) forest definition into CFBE-related sectors, especially forest carbon under REDD+ and bioenergy, has had a detrimental impact (see Section 5.2.3). The UNFCCC definition enables an approach to forest waste residue definitions that maximise extraction of materials to be used to, for example, for bioenergy. Emphasis on a forest's ecological integrity, as adopted in the Convention on Biological Diversity (CBD), is not prioritised and, where it is included, is as a co-benefit.

The circular plastics and CFBE case studies underline a need to make the link between how each sector defines materials and waste, and waste law more generally. The prevalent definition of waste used in legalisation around the world, based on intent to discard, is often perceived to be a barrier to its reuse, recycling, and recovery (see Section 1.3.1). In practice, however, the definition of waste seems to not have blocked the implementation of circular practices (Steenmans 2018). Definitional challenges of 'waste' within the plastics and the CFBE sectors are yet to receive significant attention from law and policy researchers.

6.3 Prevention, Reuse, Recycling, and Recovery

Despite prevention often being the prioritised waste management strategy at international and national levels (e.g., Basel Convention, Art. 4(2)(a)[1]; Waste Framework Directive 2008/98/EC, Art. 4), CE and the law are in practice predominantly focused on measures to promote recycling and, to lesser degree, other recovery. Measures on waste recycling and recovery dominate explicitly labelled CE laws, though laws underpinning CE principles do include more support for prevention measures, such as right to repair laws promoting reduced obsolescence of products (see Section 2.3.2). Despite potential for the incorporation of waste prevention within laws underpinning CE principles, the ways in which such measures are usually implemented still skew towards recycling and other recovery. The absence of preventive approaches and a substitute focus instead on recycling and recovery are observed in both circular plastics and CFBE practices.

Plastic use is predominantly linear, as it is often cheaper to make new plastics rather than recycling them. This is especially the case with chemical recycling (Parker 2020). Where plastics are recycled or recovered in another way, such as waste-to-energy for district heating, there are risks of commodification and lock-ins to systems reliant on, and thereby promoting, continued plastics consumption and subsequent generation of their wastes. Yet if prevention was immediately promoted through measures such as bans, there may be harmful consequences for, for example, the informal recycling sector, which relies on continued plastic waste generation. This example illustrates the misalignment that can be found between bottom-up and top-down approaches to circular plastics. Any law or policy actions need to consider the full life cycle of plastics and their environmental and social consequences, including justice implications for all actors involved across the life cycle.

The concept of cascading materials is fundamental to a regenerative closed-loop CFBE (Bezama 2016). There are, however, degrees of cascading. A manufactured product could be used once for its g intended primary use, and then used for bioenergy. Such a cascade of use would feature low on the waste hierarchy as the intention is currently incorporated into the life cycle chain to reuse or recycle the manufactured product. Higher level cascading would deliberately promote symbiotic relations between material users throughout the life cycle that maximise use value. In such cases, materials could be designed purposefully for circular reuse and recovery. Circular by design would also prioritise reducing material demand by extending the life of the product.

It is evident from the CFBE case study that the cascading concept is far from sufficiently established across all the related sectors to achieve CE. Market dynamics, fostered by climate and energy-related law and policy in many instances, are operating independently and creating niche supply chains. If cascading within a CFBE is to be successful, a comprehensive systems approach will need to be adopted, underpinned by laws and policies across the forest-related and land use sectors. This will be challenging in a sector with so many small- and medium-sized enterprises, as well as indigenous and community forestry sectors globally. Key factors that relate to cascading are sustainability and scale.

6.4 Sustainable Development

There is an assumption that any CE will by default result in sustainable development. As noted in Chapters 1 and 3 (see Sections 1.3.3 and 3.1, respectively), the claim is highly disputed and current research evidently suggests this is not the case (e.g., Blum et al. 2020). Across CEs to date a 'same-but-circular-business' model approach dominates. The emphasis remains on the economic rather than the environmental and social pillars of sustainable development. So much so that some even argue that the CE as a concept is in danger of being appropriated by big multinational companies that have already developed global supply chains (Mavropoulos 2016; Mavropoulos and Nilsen 2020). Within a 'same-but-circular-business' model approach, asking questions about transforming fundamental norms and values are not seen as relevant. The priority of companies is maximising growth while trying to offset environmental costs, and to a far lesser extent social impacts. The core issue is consumption. The 2015 Sustainable Development Goals (SDGs) recognised that sustainable development requires an integrated approach, in which consumption is also targeted. Both case studies demonstrate a failure to address sustainable development in an integrated way, especially in relation to consumption.

Within the plastic waste context, much focus remains on developing products to replace the current dominant types of plastics or increase their recyclability and recoverability. The emphasis is, therefore, on solution-based measures that continue to perpetuate current business models and result in sustainable development issues. Both bottom-up and top-down approaches are centred around solution rather than problem-based measures. Bottom-up initiatives by the informal recycling sector and private sector actors for the purposes of industrial symbiosis deal with plastic wastes that have already been generated instead of focusing on the consumption issues. Plastic wastes can provide income generation for both the informal recycling sector and within industrial symbiosis, so there is no incentive to reduce its generation. Top-down governance could present more opportunities, but again the current measures reviewed in Chapter 4 fail at present to sufficiently engage with why plastics are being consumed. Understanding this will be key to minimising plastic wastes. Consumption issues should therefore be at the forefront of any global agreement on plastics.

As demonstrated in Chapter 5, sustainable forest management is a concept that dates to the late 18th century. The concept's principles and criteria have altered over time, but the underlying goal remains the same: to extract as much value from a forest without undermining the long-term commercial value. Each of the two examples featured in the CFBE case study – forest carbon, and bioenergy – illustrated the priority given to commercial market-based approaches. Criteria to ensure sustainability are negotiated for each sector separately. There is no interconnected systemic approach across the sectors, neither spatially nor temporally. The cascading principle is not embedded into the CFBE. The result of such a fragmented regulatory approach is that it is impossible to achieve a sustainable CFBE.

6.5 Scale

As with all economic systems, CEs will operate at different scales at the micro, meso, and/or macro levels. The multilevel examples have also demonstrated the complexity of CEs, as each level across each sector has different social, environmental, and economic impacts. The taxation measures provided for in Mexico's General Circular Economy

Law, for example, are intended to incentivise circular behaviour, yet also impact the informal recycling sector (see Chapter 2). Some of their vulnerabilities were highlighted in Chapter 4. Sectors' scales are determined by numerous factors including how capital intensive the industry, proximity to virgin materials, supply chain logistics, and market demand profile, as well as investment and finance availability. Law, regulations, and standards are also factors that can have a determining effect on the commercial viability of different CE scales. Plastics and the CFBE sectors' profiles differ in many ways (plastics' manufacturing direct dependence on hydrocarbon industries being the most notable), yet also share some characteristics.

Plastics, for example, can be used within local industrial symbiosis networks that link to the transnational movement of wastes for recycling purposes. Simultaneously, plastics could leak from this system and form part of the informal recycling sector. These links together arguably could constitute a global CE. While such a global CE could achieve certain economic benefits, there would be numerous detrimental environmental and social consequences. Developing and adopting a heuristic, like the 3:2 heuristic used for industrial symbiosis systems (see Section 1.3.4), could at least help address some of the limitations of the current boundary-less CE concept. A 3:2 requirement would reduce 'same-but-circular-business' models, as businesses engaging in one recycling or recovery stream would not be able to label the practice as circular.

Given the range of needs at each scale, a mix of regulatory measures and policy interventions is needed. There is no silver bullet. Attempting to get top-down regulations ready can lead to unnecessary delays in action. REDD+ was a prime example of a top-down measure under the UNFCCC to mitigate climate change in forests through establishing a market-based mechanism. Enormous amounts of resources, money, and time were invested, primarily by developed countries and international financial organisations, into agreeing common reporting standards and rules for REDD+ for over a decade. If the same resources were made available to indigenous peoples and forest-based communities at the micro scale, without a market mechanism being needed, more progress could have been made. The same concerns are already being raised about Bioenergy Carbon Capture and Storage (BECCS) with again top-down measures being promoted under the UNFCCC. This is a concern that is shared with an international treaty on plastics. Progress will be slow, and it will be several years before a treaty is agreed upon and enters into force. National and subnational level action is therefore required, as plastic wastes are a crucial issue that needs to be dealt with now.

6.6 Social Equity

The inclusion of social equity, not only to benefit current generations but also future generations, is fundamental to how the CE is to be developed, as is the role that law and policy-makers will play. By placing social equity at the forefront of devising laws and policies for a CE, there will be a need for an understanding of why existing inequities occur: how does law enable the persistence of historically embedded injustices to continue unchallenged? In the case studies, we uncovered to some degree the important role that law has played in creating and sustaining injustices. They also provided insights into the potential injustices that future generations would face if laws designed to enable a CE do not address justice issues from the outset.

There are multiple intergenerational and intragenerational issues evident with plastics waste. Plastics consumed today that leak into the natural environment will remain for decades, even centuries in some cases, and have an impact on human well-being. There are multiple layers to the intragenerational issues including current transnational movement of plastic wastes as a result of waste colonialism, resulting in displacing polluting impacts of plastic waste management from the Global North to the Global South; and waste operations sited near poor and marginalised communities. Meanwhile, procedural processes are not open and transparent resulting in those stakeholders most impacted, particularly the informal recycling sector, being inadequately involved within law and policy-making on plastic waste regulation. In relation to the latter, even where informal workers are being recognised more, this has been detrimental. Mexico's General Circular Economy Law, for example, recognises the informal recycling sector but formalisation has negative tax consequences for workers (see Section 2.3.1).

Weber et al. (2019) have proposed the concept of 'waste justice'. Waste justice specifically addresses an increasing range of global issues caused by waste production and disposal. For example, waste justice highlights the growing contamination of livelihoods of indigenous people and communities, and the progressive pollution of areas traditionally considered pristine (Weber et al. 2019). Waste justice is 'a new and growing social movement that includes a variety of progressive political, economic and ecological currents, aside from grassroots initiatives, campaigning to minimize and eventually eliminate waste as a by-product of our non-circular modes of production' (Weber et al. 2019). Movements focusing on waste justice could bring attention to the problem in a similar manner to those who have highlighted the concept of waste colonialism.

The CFBE case study highlights the challenges within the forestry sector to address social equity problems and ensure that current and future generations benefit from law and policy interventions. Historically indigenous peoples have been the victims of violence, losing land to expropriation for agriculture expansion, conservation areas, and infrastructure such as dams and to meet the demand for timber in importing countries. These trends continue today with forest and land defenders experiencing the highest rates of violence and death amongst human rights defenders around the world (Global Witness 2021).

The CFBE case study reveals that the UNFCCC is only superficially addressing social justice issues within the forestry sector. The main UNFCCC forest mechanism, REDD+, is seen to perpetuate distributional injustices, especially considering differential historical contributions to climate change. REDD+ is primarily a market-based mechanism which allows polluting industries, such as aviation, to purchase emission reduction credits to offset their own emissions. It is further commodification of forest lands ruling from the adoption of BECCS policies, along with the drive to increase the use of timber materials in construction will add pressure to dismiss claims for customary land rights from forest communities and indigenous peoples to be dismissed by statutory authorities in reference for allocating concession contracts to foreign companies. Ongoing recognition injustices will not only impact current forest peoples' and indigenous peoples' generations whose cultures will be decimated, but they will further cause irrevocable harm to future generations as knowledge and alternative ways of understanding the world are lost.

6.7 Conclusion

Observations from plastic wastes and the forest BE, examined in Chapters 4 and 5, respectively, highlight limitations of current laws and policies on CEs. Many are common challenges across both sectors that necessitate further attention if systems are to become truly circular. The challenges include:

1 Legal definitions are an issue. There is a need for clearer links between how each sector defines materials and waste, and waste law more generally.
2 The linear economic system dominates throughout the sectors and is still enabled by a focus on recycling and other recovery

operations in practice instead of prevention (in opposition to the waste hierarchy). The ways in which these recycling and recovery operations are currently implemented risk their commodification and lock-ins to unsustainable, non-circular, and unjust systems.

3 Sustainable development is not a given outcome of circular approaches. In both sectors, many of the measures adopted to facilitate circularity have, for example, detrimental equity and justice implications.

4 Equity and justice issues are critically predominant. As different approaches, measures, and perspectives have been considered, equity and justice issues permeated discussions.

Shifting the focus to equity and justice issues within the CE concept will go a long way in addressing the areas requiring further research. Current CEs perpetuate business-as-usual models, which overlook justice issues and impacts. This is one of the dominant factors why circular approaches are as yet not just, sustainable, nor fair.

Note

1 The Basel Convention does not implement a waste hierarchy. The first general obligation beyond the prohibition of certain imports and exports of hazardous wastes is that each Party 'shall take the appropriate measures to: (a) Ensure that the generation of hazardous wastes and other wastes within it is reduced to a minimum, taking into account social, technological and economy aspects' (Basel Convention, Art. 4(2)(a)).

References

Bezama, A. 2016. Let us discuss how cascading can help implement the circular economy and the bio-economy strategies. *Waste Management and Research*, 34(7), pp.593–594. https://doi.org/10.1177/0734242X16657973.

Blum, N.U., Haupt, M. and Bening, C.R. 2020. Why "circular" doesn't always mean "sustainable". *Resources, Conservation and Recycling*, 162, p.105042. https://doi.org/10.1016/j.resconrec.2020.105042.

Global Witness. 2021. Last line of defence: the industries causing the climate crisis against land and environmental defenders. www.globalwitness.org/en/campaigns/environmental-activists/last-line-defence/.

Kirchherr J., Reike, D. and Hekkert, M. 2017. Conceptualizing the circular economy: an analysis of 114 definitions. *Resources, Conservation and Recycling*, 127, pp.221–232. https://doi.org/10.1016/j.resconrec.2017.09.005.

Mavropoulos, A. 2016. Shaping the social footprint of circular economy. *Wasteless Future*. https://wastelessfuture.com/shaping-the-social-footprint-of-circular-economy/.

Mavropoulos, A. and Nilsen, A.W. 2020. *Industry 4.0 and Circular Economy: Towards a Wasteless Future or a Wasteful Planet?* Wiley.

Parker, L. 2020. An old-school plan to fight plastic pollution gathers steam. *National Geographic.* www.nationalgeographic.com/science/article/old-school-plan-to-fight-plastic-pollution-gathers-steam.

Steenmans, K. 2018. *Enabling Industrial Symbiosis through Regulations, Policies and Property Rights.* PhD Thesis. University of Surrey, UK.

Weber, G., Cabras, I., Calaf-Forn, M., Puig-Ventosa, I. and D'Alisa, G. 2019. Promoting waste degrowth and environmental justice at a local level: the case of unit-pitching schemes in Spain. *Ecological Economics*, 156, pp.306–317. https://doi.org/10.1016/j.ecolecon.2018.09.024.

7 Conclusions and Future Research Landscape

The concept of a circular economy (CE) has rapidly gained support from all quarters: government, business, and civil society. The concept's simplicity, and the promissory values associated with it, makes it highly appealing. However, as this book set out the CE is a complex mosaic of multiple intertwined themes, topics, and layers. This complex mosaic includes the law and the role it has in establishing CE transitions. The question that led us in researching this book was whether justice issues are within the existing frame of CE law and policy.

7.1 Introduction

We began this book by introducing the CE's origins as a concept and outlined its constitutive dimensions. In Chapter 1, we used Kirchherr et al.'s (2017) conceptual framing to set out five key themes of a CE: waste; prevention, reuse, recycling, and recovery of materials and waste; sustainable development; scale; and social equity for the benefit of current and future generations. Throughout the book, these five themes served as the framing for our investigations of CE-related laws and policies.

We argue that Kirchherr et al.'s (2017) inclusion of social equity in their CE conceptual frame is a fundamental conception to be mirrored in future legal and policy research. Social equity for current and future generations should be at the centre of legal and policy research on CE creation and implementation, and not at their periphery as it is currently.

Laws used to advance transitions to CEs were set out and discussed in Chapter 2. Our review argues that current law for CEs often supports the status quo rather than drives any transformation. Part of the issue is the impossibility for waste management to be truly circular

DOI: 10.4324/9780429355141-7

within a linear economic system (Kovacic et al. 2019b; Viva et al. 2020). One of the promises of CE is that it will result in the decoupling of economic growth from resource use, but this is wishful thinking. In the case of weak CE, where many products are designed or redesigned to meet wants rather than needs, a producer will intend to make more of them, regardless of whether the business model is linear or circular (Hart and Pomponi 2021). Such a weak CE model would perpetuate failed attempts to decouple economic growth from resource extraction and use, never sufficiently reducing demand pressures on the Earth's systems or addressing underlying distributive injustices (Velenturf and Purnell 2021). There is thus a need to change the economic system, but, despite increasing degrowth and other socio-ecological transformation approaches proposed (e.g., Schmelzer et al. 2022), there is insufficient traction for such systemic change.

We presented our case in Chapter 3 to expand research on CE law and policies to bring justice dimensions into their frame. Research on law reflects a broader pattern within CE research of failing to adopt a systems-wide approach. The outcome from not adopting a systems-wide approach in law is that the interconnections, and their implications, of interventions in specific legal domains are not considered, understood, nor recognised. This can result in unexpected, perverse outcomes from regulatory reforms being undertaken. Such perverse chains of influence result, for example, in extended producer responsibility (EPR) driving lost income opportunities for the poorest and most marginalised in the global economy, such as informal workers. Chapter 3 also highlighted the need to research and understand laws' historical roots. Many of which go back to the colonial era and the injustices they created, and many of which remain today, especially for peoples in the Global South. The concluding section of this chapter used several examples to highlight why it is necessary to identify as soon as possible, even *a priori*, potential distributional, recognition, and procedural justice issues that could result from adopting particular law and policy approaches to CE transitions.

To investigate the complex interrelationships of law, policy, and CE transitions with greater detail, two in-depth case studies were developed in Chapters 4 and 5. Chapter 4 drew on the case of circular plastic wastes. We argued that the tensions between perceptions of plastics as resources as well as pollutants confuse the alignment of bottom-up and top-down legal and policy approaches to achieving circularity within the plastics sector. Resultant justice issues from the misalignment were also highlighted through examples of bottom-up approaches (the informal recycling sector and industrial symbiosis) and discussions on developments within international and national governance of circular plastics. Chapter 5 then introduced the case of the circular forest bioeconomy (CFBE). Experiences in two sub-sectors within the CFBE shed light on some of the inconsistencies with CE principles, as well as the ways through which climate change mitigation laws are shaping priorities within large-scale policies, and some of the justice issues arisen so far under reduced emissions from deforestation and degradation (REDD+), and industrial scale bioenergy, as well as bioenergy carbon capture and storage.

For the reflection on lessons learnt about legal challenges faced from these two case studies on circular plastic wastes and CFBE, we returned in Chapter 6 to Kirchherr et al.'s (2017) conceptual CE framing. We demonstrate how each of its five key themes – waste; prevention, reuse, recycling, and recovery of materials and waste; sustainable development; scale; and social equity for the benefit of current and future generations – can be used to evaluate the current laws and policies within the two plastics and bioeconomy (BE) sectors, and consider how justice can be better incorporated into their framing.

7.2 Future Research Landscape

Law and policy-making does not happen in a vacuum. It is important to be cognizant of the potential impacts that changes in ecological, political, economic, and technological systems may have on the research landscape, however speculative. In the following section, we therefore set out the future context within which CE law and policy research will be conducted. We cover four areas – climate change, trade, governance, and digital technology – that will individually and/ or collectively determine the choices available to those designing and implementing laws and policies for CE transitions. We use the United Nations Framework Convention on Climate Change (UNFCCC) Paris Agreement 2050 target date for reaching net zero as a timeline for each of the four areas.

7.2.1 Climate Change

The Intergovernmental Panel on Climate Change (IPCC) estimates, based on nationally determined contributions submitted by parties to the 2015 Paris Agreement, that by 2050 global average surface temperatures will be 3.2°C above the average surface temperature before the industrial revolution (IPCC 2022). This will exceed by 1.7°C the Paris Agreement target of 1.5°C. A rise in temperatures at this scale will significantly increase the number of extreme weather events, both slow onset events, such as droughts, and rapid onset events, like hurricanes and flooding around the world. The burden will be disproportionately borne by small island states and least-developed countries in the Global South (IPCC 2022). The cumulative and collective impact that climate change will have on the global economic system is difficult to calculate. Suffice to say that the global economic order will need to adapt to significant disruptions, many of which are challenging to determine.

Research on transitioning to CEs and the role law plays in ensuring sustainable, equitable, and just outcomes, including for future generations, need to consider the impacts climate change will have on the global economic order at all levels from the micro to the macro. It will also need to focus on the impact that policies and measures adopted to transition to a net zero global economic system will have on justice issues.

7.2.2 Global Trade

Global trade is projected to double in real terms by 2050 to reach USD 100 trillion (UK Department for International Trade 2021). The greatest share in trade growth will come from Asian emerging economies China, India, and Indonesia. Material flows will be transformed by the growth in demand within these economies and their neighbouring countries. The UK Department for International Trade's projection does not incorporate potential future circular trade value from, for example, remanufacturing and repair, secondary raw materials, and waste. It is likely that circular trade will see material flows following a similar pattern with the greatest share increase of a growing market circulating within China, India, and Indonesia. These changes are resulting in growing concern over the security of material flows.

International trade relations are already under increasing pressure from politicised mega-regional agreements such as the Comprehensive and Progressive Agreement for a Trans-Pacific Partnership (CPTPP).[1] Adding to the regionalisation of trade relations both the coronavirus (SARS-CoV2) pandemic and the Russia-Ukraine war have sent shock waves through the global economy disrupting investment, global supply chains, and trade. Climate change is also impacting global trade not only because of more extreme weather events affecting production and distribution but also competition for raw materials, especially rare earth metals, required for technologies to transform fossil fuel-dependent economies. Circular trade law research, as noted in Chapter 3 is in its early stages and appears to be focusing on bilateral free trade agreements between developed economies such as the United Kingdom, Canada, and Australia or the World Trade Organization agreements. Given the dynamic changes occurring within global trade, and the impacts these will have for material flows in the future, research on trade law and the CE needs to evolve rapidly. Transitioning to more circular trade systems will inevitably have implications for existing equity and justice, especially for those already poor and marginalised communities under the current linear system. Researchers will not only need to keep pace with developments within the trade but also the impacts on trade relations from the geopolitical shift in economic power from the Global North to China, India, and Indonesia.

7.2.3 Governance

It is difficult to anticipate the form that global governance will take by 2050. Economic governance has for many years operated under international institutions established in the post-World War II period, such as the World Bank and the International Monetary Fund dominated since the 1990s by a neo-liberal Washington consensus that promoted deregulation, neo-liberal markets, free trade, and the rule of law. Simultaneously, the international legal order is centred upon the principle of state sovereignty, a concept whose origins come from the Treaty of Westphalia (1648), and established the United Nations after World War II in New York as its main institutional body. Yet, international governance is more than states, economics, and institutions; international governance is primarily about power and values. As China's and India's economic stars are in ascendency, along with other middle-income countries like Brazil, Indonesia, and Mexico, the dominance that the West, primarily Europe and the United States, had on international institutions, both economic and legal, is weakening. This is a trend that is likely to continue up to 2050.

The shifting sands within geopolitics over the coming three decades will have implications for priorities given to values in law and policy. State-led authoritarian regimes, such as China, Brazil, and India, have already pushed back on human rights asserting sovereignty and invoking anti-colonising rhetoric as a defence. International institutions are increasingly under scrutiny and seen to be not fit for purpose to enable global international cooperation. Critiques focus on the universalist and Western bias to the detriment of alternative worldviews, including those of indigenous peoples. Although other attacks reflect more the struggle between Western superpowers, who are losing authority, legitimacy, and power to ascending powers like China and India, and to a lesser degree Russia. Any proposal to develop an inclusive CE framework using existing international institutions and associated agreements will certainly need to navigate changing priorities by states and other non-state actors. How justice aspects fare under dynamic changes in global governance depends on whether those working for a CE commit to putting them at the centre of the frame.

7.2.4 Digital Technology

Predictions vary significantly for the number of connected devices in the world by 2050 – between 24 billion (Ericsson 2022) to 100 billion (Karunarathne et al. 2018) – but the overall trend is clear: the world is increasingly becoming more connected by digital technologies. CE advocates frequently identify increased digitalisation, including the Internet of Things (IoT), Artificial Intelligence (AI), and Big Data analytics capacity, as fundamental to rapidly upscaling circularity across sectors at all levels: micro, meso, and macro. Potentially the full life cycle flows of materials could be digitally recorded in material passports.[2] Information about origins, processing, use, and secondary markets until end-of-life processes documenting waste management could all be gathered using digital technologies.

There are numerous legal dimensions to the digital revolution as all areas of law are impacted either directly or indirectly from copyright and intellectual property rights, contracts, tort, consumer rights, to environmental laws and human rights such as right to privacy. Although there is extensive research interest in the important role that digital technologies, including blockchain (e.g., Kouhizadeh et al. 2019; Steenmans et al. 2021a), AI (e.g., Agrawal et al. 2021; Wilson et al. 2022), and the IoT (e.g., Ramadoss et al. 2018; Rejeb et al. 2022), could play in enabling a more rapid transition to a CE, there is limited legal research (Steenmans et al. 2021a, 2021b). Going forward, legal research on how digital technologies are incorporated into CE systems, and the equity and justice impacts such as access to material and wealth flows, benefit sharing, surveillance, and privacy, as well as digital exclusion and discrimination, need to be on the agenda.

7.2.5 Summary

The dynamic ecological, economic, political, and technical changes occurring over the coming decades up to 2050 and beyond provide the backdrop for the crafting and implementation of CE transition laws and policies. The geopolitical economic order is not in a stable steady state. Tensions between superpowers with stresses multiplied by climate change and related ecological impacts, such as water insecurity, will influence the decisions being made on policies and laws to enable CEs. In this section, we set out areas within the wider context to focus on as part of CE law and policy research going forward, especially as each will have a significant impact on how justice issues are framed and addressed.

7.3 Concluding Remarks

Law and policy research has yet to prioritise social justice within CEs. The lack of attention paid to social equity for current and future generations is a serious omission given that the CE is a 'last chance' for the 'current capitalistic and market-based system to become more sustainable' (Will 2019). The reasons for the present situation are evident upon closer examination not only of CE-related laws and policies but also how they are being incorporated and applied in specific sectors.

As Chapter 2 and the two case studies on plastics and the forest BE illustrate, the preferred model for CEs to be supported by laws, regulations, and policies appears to be the 'same-but-circular-business' one in which, as Will (2019) observes, transformation of capitalism is not seen to be necessary. Degrowth, which was integral to key concepts that informed the CE, is no longer a point of reference for law and policy-makers. The ongoing failure to incorporate alternatives to growth-based economic models into CE law and policy research is increasingly concerning. As Rockström et al. (2009) note, 'the thresholds in key Earth System processes exist irrespective of peoples' preferences, values or compromises based on political and socio-economic feasibility'. A paradigm shift towards a less materialistic lifestyle is taking place in niches of society, but so far and foreseeably no critical mass has been reached. Any large-scale transformation "on the fly" is unlikely to take place in the face of diverse institutional and technological path dependencies, both of which current CE-related laws and policies appear to support. Growth in and of itself, whether in a linear or a CE, may not be inimical to sustainable development within planetary boundaries (Desing et al. 2020). As long as law and governance systems are constrained to serve growth, positive developments in environmental law will fail to keep anthropogenic endeavours within ecological limits necessary for the human and non-human species survival in the long term (Garver 2019).

Under a 'same-but-circular-business' model, social justice is not embedded from the outset. Some argue, however, that social justice can be incorporated into the model along the way. Schröder et al. (2019), as highlighted in Chapter 3, claim that the 'same-but-circular-business' model can be expanded to include working with marginalised and poor communities, especially in the Global South, to deliver a transition away from linear-capitalism that is equitable and fair. However, Schroder's faith rests on an international legal order and its governance institutions that themselves are part of the problem, including environmental law (M'Gonigle and Takeda 2013). It is worth taking on board Bauwens et al.'s (2020) observation that not all pathways and outcomes to a CE will be identical or even should be identical. Efforts to pursue a standardised global CE will perpetuate a universalist approach that has its roots in colonialism and instrumentalist values.

Bringing justice into the frame for legal and policy research is an absolute necessity if future CEs are to be sustainable, inclusive, and just. Without researchers addressing questions, and finding solutions to, distributional, recognition, and procedural issues and injustices embedded within the current dominant linear economic system in any future CE. Failing to do so will also leave potentially many low- and middle-income countries, and other poor and marginalised peoples in developed countries, severed from opportunities to gain from the economic, social, and environmental benefits CEs could hold.

This book has taken the initial steps to incorporate justice discourse within CE law and policy research. In this book, we have documented the limits to increasing circularity in specific sectors (see Chapters 4 and 5) within the linear economy's legal architecture, while also showing how laws for a CE could have negative distributional, recognition, and procedural justice impacts if not designed appropriately (see Chapter 3). In the final analysis, a research framework to direct CE legal research towards questions relating to distributional, recognition, and procedural justice was put forward. We further added thematic areas which will in the coming decades have a determining influence on the context within which CEs laws and policies will take shape. The research presented in this book is only the start of a process to bring justice into the frame on law, policy, and CEs. The process needs to pick up speed quickly if CEs are not to end up being, as Preston et al. (2019) warned, 'superficial and tokenistic ultimately failing to deliver in terms of systemic change'.

Notes

1 The Comprehensive and Progressive Agreement for Trans-Pacific Partnership, also known as TPP11 or TPP-11, is a trade agreement between Australia, Brunei, Canada, Chile, Japan, Malaysia, Mexico, New Zealand, Peru, Singapore, and Vietnam, which was signed on 8 March 2018.

2 There is much-emerging research, for example, on the use of material passports for buildings within the construction sector (e.g., Honic et al. 2019; Kovacic et al. 2019a).

References

Agrawal, R., Wankhede, V.A., Kumar, A., Luthra, S., Majumdar, A. and Kazancoglu, Y. 2021. An exploratory state-of-the-art review of artificial intelligence applications in circular economy using structural topic modelling. *Operations Management Research.* https://doi.org/10.1007/s12063-021-00212-0.

Bauwens, T., Hekkert, M. and Kirchherr, J. 2020 Circular futures: what will they look like? *Ecological Economics, 175,* p.106703. https://doi.org/10.1016/j.ecolecon.2020.106703.

Desing, H., Brunner, D., Takacs, F., Nahrath, S., Frankenberger, K. and Hischier, R. 2020. A circular economy within the planetary boundaries: towards a resource-based, systemic approach. *Resources, Conservation and Recycling, 155,* p.104673. https://doi.org/10.1016/j.resconrec.2019.104673.

Ericsson. 2022. *Why the IoT Changes Everything.* www.ericsson.com/en/internet-of-things#:~:text=By%202050%2C%20there%20will%20be,%2C%20%20elevators%2C%20even%20gym%20vests.

Garver, G. 2019. A systems-based tool for transitioning to law for a mutually enhancing human-earth relationship. *Ecological Economics, 157,* pp.165–174. https://doi.org/10.1016/j.ecolecon.2018.09.022.

Hart, J. and Pomponi, F. 2021. A circular economy: where will it take us? *Circular Economy and Sustainability,* 1, pp.127–141. https://doi.org/10.1007/s43615-021-00013-4.

Honic, M., Kovacic, I. and Rechberger, H. 2019. BIM-based material passport (MP) as an optimization tool for increasing the recyclability of buildings. *Applied Mechanics and Materials,* 887, pp.327–334. https://doi.org/10.4028/www.scientific.net/AMM.887.327.

IPCC. 2022. In: *Climate Change 2022: Impacts, Adaptation and Vulnerability. Contribution of Working Group II to the Sixth Assessment Report of the Intergovernmental Panel on Climate Change* [Pörtner, H.-O., Roberts, D.C., Tignor, M., Poloczanska E.S. et al. (Eds.)]. Cambridge University Press. https://doi.org/10.1017/9781009325844.

Karunarathne, G.G.K.W.M.S.I.R., Kulawansa, K.A.D.T. and Firdhous, M.F.M. 2018. Wireless communication technologies in internet of things: a critical evaluation. In: *International Conference on Intelligent and Innovative*

Computing Applications (ICONIC), pp.1–5. https://doi.org/10.1109/ICONIC.2018.8601226.

Kirchherr J., Reike, D. and Hekkert, M. 2017. Conceptualizing the circular economy: an analysis of 114 definitions. *Resources, Conservation and Recycling*, 127, pp.221–232. https://doi.org/10.1016/j.resconrec.2017.09.005.

Kouhizadeh, M., Sarkis, J. and Zhu, Q. 2019. At the nexus of blockchain technology, the circular economy, and product deletion. *Applied Sciences*, 9(8), p.1712. https://doi.org/10.3390/app9081712.

Kovacic, I., Honic, M. and Rechberger, H. 2019a. Proof of concept for a BIM-based material passport. In: Mutis, I. and Hartmann, T. (Eds.), *Advances in Informatics and Computing in Civil and Construction Engineering*. Springer. https://doi.org/10.1007/978-3-030-00220-6_89.

Kovacic, Z., Strand, R. and Völker, T. 2019b. *The Circular Economy in Europe: Critical Perspectives on Policies and Imaginaries*. Routledge.

M'Gonigle, M. and Takeda, L. 2013. The liberal limits of environmental law: a green legal critique. *Pace Environmental Law Review*, 30 (3), pp.1005–1115.

Preston, F., Lehne, J. and Wellesley, L. 2019. *An Inclusive Circular Economy: Priorities for Developing Countries*. The Royal Institute of International Affairs. www.chathamhouse.org/2019/05/inclusive-circular-economy.

Ramadoss, T.S., Alam, H. and Seeram, R. 2018. Artificial intelligence and Internet of Things enabled circular economy. *The International Journal of Engineering and Science*, 7(9), pp.55–63. https://doi.org/10.9790/1813-0709035563.

Rejeb, A. Suhaiza, Z., Rejeb, K., Seuring, S. and Treiblmaier, H. 2022. The Internet of Things and the circular economy: a systematic literature review and research agenda. *Journal of Cleaner Production*, 350, p.131439. https://doi.org/10.1016/j.jclepro.2022.131439.

Rockström, J., Steffen, W., Noone, K., Persson, Å, Chapin, F. S., Lambin, E. and Foley, J. 2009. Planetary boundaries: exploring the safe operating space for humanity. *Ecology and Society*, 14(2), pp.32–66. https://doi.org/10.5751/ES-03180-140232.

Schmelzer, M., Vetter, A. and Vansintjan, A. 2022. *The Future is Degrowth: A Guide to a World beyond Capitalism*. Verso.

Schröder, P. Bengtsson, M., Cohen, M. Dewick, P., Hofstetter, J. and Sarkis, J. 2019. Degrowth within –aligning circular economy and strong sustainability narratives. *Resources, Conservation and Recycling*, 146, pp.190–191. https://doi.org/10.1016/j.resconrec.2019.03.038.

Steenmans, K., Taylor, P. and Steenmans, I. 2021a. Blockchain technology for governance of plastic waste management: where are we? *Social Sciences*, 10(11), p.434. https://doi.org/10.3390/socsci10110434.

Steenmans, K., Taylor, P. and Steenmans, I. 2021b. Regulatory opportunities and challenges for blockchain adoption for circular economies. In: *2021 IEEE International Conference on Blockchain*. https://doi.org/10.1109/Blockchain53845.2021.00086.

UK Department for International Trade. 2021. *Global Trade Outlook.* https:// assets.publishing.service.gov.uk/government/uploads/system/uploads/ attachment_data/file/1036243/global-trade-outlook-september-2021.pdf.

Velenturf, A.P. and Purnell, P. 2021. Principles for a sustainable circular economy. *Sustainable Production and Consumption, 27,* pp.1437–1457. https://doi.org/10.1016/j.spc.2021.02.018.

Viva, L., Ciulli, F., Kolk, A. and Rothenberg, G. 2020. Designing circular waste management strategies: the case of organic waste in Amsterdam. *Advanced Sustainable Systems,* 4(9), pp.1–17. https://doi.org/10.1002/adsu. 202000023.

Will, M. 2019. Towards a sustainable circular economy – remarks on plastics and wood-waste sector. *The Central European Review of Economics and Management,* 3(4), pp.149–183. https://doi.org/10.29015/cerem.862.

Wilson, M., Paschen, J. and Pitt, L. 2022. The circular economy meets artificial intelligence (AI): understanding the opportunities of AI for reverse logistics. *Management of Environmental Quality,* 33(1), pp.9–25. https://doi. org/10.1108/MEQ-10-2020-0222.

Index

Note: **Bold** page numbers refer to tables; *Italic* page numbers refer to figures and page numbers followed by "n" denote endnotes.

Printed in the United States
by Baker & Taylor Publisher Services